Orient Express

Orient Express
Silvena Rowe

Photographs by Jonathan Lovekin

Interlink Books

An imprint of Interlink Publishing Group, Inc.
Northampton, Massachusetts

Contents

To Mama

How fair is thy love, my sister, my spouse! how much better is thy love than wine!
and the smell of thine ointments than all spices!

Thy lips, O my spouse, drop as the honeycomb: honey and milk are under thy tongue;
and the smell of thy garments is like the smell of Lebanon.

A garden inclosed is my sister, my spouse; a spring shut up, a fountain sealed.

Thy plants are an orchard of pomegranates, with pleasant fruits; camphire,
with spikenard,

Spikenard and saffron; calamus and cinnamon, with all trees of frankincense;
myrrh and aloes, with all the chief spices.

The Song of Solomon 4:10–14

Introduction

My father used to read to me from an old copy of *One Thousand and One Nights*. I would listen, enthralled, as he gave voice to the ancient Persian stories and folk tales. My imagination ran wildly through the treasures of the bazaars and spice markets that the characters inhabited. To my young self, none of it seemed all that far removed from reality, as my father was descended from a long line of aristocratic Turks and I'd grown up eating the sort of dishes the sultans of the stories would have enjoyed. The flavors of those markets were never far from my palate.

Of course, to me it was just the food of my childhood, and one of the joys of living with a father whose rich cultural heritage—that of the Ottoman Empire—was so culinarily obsessed. It is the food that I have always loved most, that I have taken with me on whatever journey I have embarked upon, and that I have never forgotten.

Food and stories have always gone hand in hand for me. In *Purple Citrus & Sweet Perfume* I traveled extensively through the Eastern Mediterranean, listened to the storyteller Hakawati Abu Shadi, made new friends, and, of course, discovered a host of exciting dishes and cooking methods, some of which I hope to have passed to you.

Orient Express is the next chapter in my long love affair with the cuisine of the Eastern Mediterranean. My inspiration for this book came from the street foods that can be found on almost every corner of every town and city. Istanbul, Ankara, and Gaziantep, Beirut, Damascus and Aleppo, Cairo, and Amman. In these places, the food is enjoyed for its simplicity and ease by people standing where it was bought, or perching on a wall to gather, eat, and talk. From gözleme and börek, to pilaf and shawarma, all are served with the generous, warm hospitality of the Eastern Mediterranean people. Always sharing, always giving, even when they have little for themselves. I was always made to feel welcome.

For me, this aspect of Eastern Mediterranean cuisine epitomizes where East meets West. It hints at the flavors of the Orient, while embracing modern life. Food that is exotic and vibrant, but so simple and easy to prepare—perfect for sharing with friends.

As with *Purple Citrus & Sweet Perfume*, the originating theme of these dishes is still very much Ottoman, but also blended in with my very modern take on this heritage are some Arabian notes, evoking the many spices that traditionally crossed the trade routes from east to west. The spices used in the Eastern Mediterranean are generally subtler than in other cuisines, never too fierce or overpowering. Ginger, cumin, cardamom, and cinnamon can be found in both savory and sweet preparations, added not just for flavor but also for aroma.

I believe that the spices in *Orient Express* encapsulate the feeling of ease, that unhurried atmosphere of the Eastern Mediterranean that I've grown to love so much. Like east and west, exotic and calm, mystical and yet so simple, the recipes I've created in this book are full of contrasts highlighting the unique sweet and sour flavors of Eastern Mediterranean cuisine. Za'atar and saffron, chili and cumin, sumac and fresh herbs, cardamom and honey, orange blossom and lemon balm. Vivid colors, wonderful scents, irresistible flavors: a feast for every sense and every gathering.

Orient Express is all about sharing, so I've designed recipes that will serve six or eight smaller dishes, allowing you to dip in and out of the five flavor-themed chapters and create your very own Eastern Mediterranean feast. For a light lunch serving 6–8 people, choose 4 or 5 recipes (depending on your guests' appetites!). So invite a few friends, get comfortable, share some stories, and enjoy the food…

Chef's Note

At the end of this book I've included an **essential accompaniments and spice blends** section. It includes my own simple recipes for Eastern Mediterranean essentials such as **za'atar** and **baharat**, as well as easy instructions for making **pomegranate molasses**, another Eastern Mediterranean cooking staple. There's also a section on the Eastern Mediterranean pantry, which suggests some staples needed for the recipes in this book and explains some of the more unusual ingredients.

All **herbs** listed in the ingredients are dried and ground, unless otherwise stated. When I refer to a large or small bunch of fresh herbs this is a rough guide to what you'll be able to find in your grocery store—when using fresh herbs, most of the time you can use as much as you wish to bring the flavor out. When a smaller quantity is required for a more subtle flavor I've indicated that you use a 2oz/50g pack instead, which I find is the standard size available in supermarkets.

When it comes to **olive oil**, I always use the best-quality extra virgin oil I can find, as this will always have the most satisfying flavor. But it's fine to use whatever olive oil you have at hand. I also often recommend cooking with clarified butter (ghee), which is bought in liquid form and doesn't burn as easily or turn brown.

I **season** a lot of my dishes with freshly ground sea salt and black pepper. Always use as little or as much as suits your tastes.

Finally, **cooking times** are shown in degrees Farenheit or centigrade (for fan-assisted ovens). For non-fan-assisted ovens, add 20 degrees to the temperature indicated.

Emerald Spice & Gold Dust

ZA'ATAR AND SAFFRON

Za'atar (pronounced za-ah-ta) is a blend of herbs and spices used in cooking throughout the Eastern Mediterranean region. Many chefs have their own secret recipes and, no matter how hard you try (and believe me, I've tried everything), they will never divulge it to you.

In general it is made up of ground sumac, toasted sesame seeds, and dried green herbs, usually thyme and oregano, which give it that rich emerald color. The flavor is hard to describe because with so many "secret" ingredients, it can be tangy, zesty, or nutty.

Making your own za'atar at home is simple. I have my own favorite blend, named after my new restaurant, Quince (see page 180), but if you don't have time, it is available to buy ready-blended. Za'atar can be used to flavor lamb or chicken, it can be sprinkled on roasted vegetables and pastries, and it can even be mixed with a little olive oil and drizzled on bread.

Saffron comes from the saffron crocus flower and is made by drying the tiny threads of the flower's stigmas. It is, quite literally, like gold dust, as it's the most expensive spice (by weight) in the world, more expensive than gold. Fortunately, when cooking with saffron, less is more. Crushed and soaked in warm water or white wine for at least five minutes, only a few threads will make a huge difference. And the deep golden yellow color is something to behold when creating dishes.

The unique floral yet slightly bitter taste of saffron works particularly well in homemade mayonnaise and aioli, or when combined with cumin and mellow paprika. But never be tempted to use too much, as it can overpower a dish and leave it with a slightly medicinal taste.

Spiced Quail and Foie Gras Filo Parcels

These wonderful cute and tasty pies are not dissimilar to those known as bisteeya in North Africa. Fast food at its best, you can also make these with chicken or pigeon. It's one of my signature dishes for my Quince chef's table.

4 quails, approx. 7oz/200g each

3 tablespoons olive oil

2 shallots, sliced

2 garlic cloves, crushed

1in/2cm fresh ginger, peeled and finely chopped

6 saffron threads

½ teaspoon ground cumin

½ teaspoon chili flakes

3 tablespoons/40ml cognac or brandy

1 cup/250ml chicken stock

small bunch of fresh thyme with flowers, chopped

10 sheets of filo pastry (standard supermarket-bought size)

3oz/100g fresh foie gras, cubed

3oz/100g pistachios, toasted and finely chopped

1½ tablespoons melted butter

3 tablespoons confectioner's sugar

Preheat the oven to 400°F (350°F fan)/200°C (180°C fan).

Wash the quails and pat them dry with a clean cloth. Separate the legs from the breasts and season the pieces. In a large heavy pan, sauté all the quail pieces in the olive oil on high heat for 2–3 minutes, browning on all sides. Add the shallots, garlic, ginger, saffron, cumin, and chili flakes. Reduce the heat and add the cognac, taking care not to set it alight. Finally, stir in the stock. Cover and cook on low to medium heat for 45 minutes, until the quail is tender. Remove from heat and allow to cool.

Put aside the cooking juices. Remove the meat from the quail pieces and discard the bones and skin. Shred the meat and place in a bowl. Return the cooking liquid to medium heat and simmer for another 10–15 minutes, until the liquid has reduced to a quarter. Now stir in the fresh thyme and shredded meat, season, and cook for a final 2–3 minutes.

Lay out a sheet of filo pastry (you need sheets that are approx. 8 × 12in/ 20 × 10cm in size). Lay a second sheet on top of the first. Cut the two layers in half so you're left with two double-thick squares. Repeat with the remaining 8 filo sheets until you have 10 squares in total. Brush with a little melted butter and in the center of each square place a generous spoonful of the quail mixture, top with a cube of the foie gras, and finally sprinkle with some chopped pistachios. Fold in the corners of each square to make 10 small parcels.

Arrange the parcels on a baking sheet, seam side down. Brush the tops with the melted butter and bake for 10–12 minutes, until golden. Remove and dust with the confectioner's sugar.

Makes 10

Baby Carrot, Orange, and Za'atar Hummus

1lb/450g baby carrots, peeled

1 large onion, sliced

3 garlic cloves, crushed

4 tablespoons olive oil

3 tablespoons orange juice

zest of 1 orange

1 tablespoon za'atar

3 teaspoons ground cumin

1 tablespoon tahini

TO SERVE

1 teaspoon tahini

2 tablespoons canned chickpeas, drained

Preheat the oven to 425°F (400°F fan)/220°C (200°C fan).

Spread out the carrots, onions, and garlic in an ovenproof dish, drizzle with olive oil, and add a cup of water. Cover the dish with foil and roast the vegetables for 25–30 minutes, until cooked. Remove the vegetables from the oven and allow to cool.

Place the cooked vegetables in a food processor. Add the orange juice, orange zest, za'atar, cumin, and tahini. Process until smooth and season to taste.

Spoon into a serving bowl, drizzle with the extra tahini, and sprinkle the chickpeas on top.

For 6 to share

Börek Rolls with Crab, Saffron, and Fennel

I love crab and I love börek, so this is my ideal snack! Börek, a Turkish stuffed pastry, is traditionally prepared with meat, offal, or vegetables, but using fresh white crabmeat, perfumed with a touch of saffron, makes this a thoroughly modern sultan of böreks.

11oz/300g	fresh white crabmeat, cooked
2–3	fresh tarragon sprigs, finely chopped
1	large fennel bulb, finely sliced
6	scallions, finely sliced
2	tablespoons olive oil
6	saffron threads, crushed
½	teaspoon ground sumac
½	teaspoon brown sugar
	zest of 1 lemon
	juice of ½ lemon
12	sheets of filo pastry + extra in case they break
2	tablespoons melted butter
½	teaspoon ground sumac (extra, for garnish)

Preheat the oven to 400°F (350°F fan)/200°C (180°C fan).

Place the cooked crabmeat in a bowl, add the tarragon, cover, and refrigerate until needed.

In a pan, sauté the sliced fennel and scallions in the olive oil on low to medium heat for 15 minutes. Add the saffron, sumac, and sugar. Season and cook for a further 3–4 minutes, until the fennel is caramelized and still moist. Stir in the lemon zest and juice and remove from the heat. Allow to cool, then add the crabmeat and tarragon, combine well, and season again, if required.

Use one sheet of filo pastry for each börek cigar. Fold into thirds, so that you have a thin rectangle about 4in/10cm wide. Brush with a little melted butter and spoon some of the filling onto one end. Roll once to seal in the filling. Fold in the sides and continue to roll (as if making a spring roll). Repeat with the remaining pastry sheets and filling. Arrange the rolls on a baking sheet, seam side down. Brush the tops with the remaining butter and sprinkle with sumac. Bake in the oven for 10–20 minutes, until golden brown.

Makes 12

Za'atar Spiced Rabbit Gözleme

Gözleme are a favorite in Turkey, a sort of pastry sandwich, sold everywhere from street corners to sophisticated restaurants and usually prepared with local cheese or lamb. For something more distinctive I love to make them with rabbit.

2 tablespoons olive oil

1 large onion, sliced

3 garlic cloves, crushed

1 rabbit, jointed into small pieces

1 teaspoon ground cumin

1 teaspoon ground paprika

½ teaspoon ground allspice

¼ teaspoon ground cardamom

1 teaspoon za'atar, plus extra for garnish

scant ½ cup/100ml dry white wine

¾ cup/200ml chicken stock

small bunch of fresh oregano, finely chopped

3 tablespoons melted butter

3 tablespoons olive oil (extra)

3 large circular sheets of yufka or filo pastry

1–2 tablespoons melted clarified butter or ghee

Preheat the oven to 400°F (350°F fan)/200°C (180°C fan).

Heat the olive oil in a large ovenproof casserole dish. Add the onion, garlic, and rabbit pieces and cook for about 5 minutes, until the meat is browned on all sides. Stir in the cumin, paprika, allspice, cardamom, za'atar, white wine, and chicken stock. Simmer for 5 minutes, then cover and cook in the oven for 45 minutes.

Remove the rabbit from the casserole dish and allow to cool completely before shredding the meat and discarding the skin and bones. Meanwhile, return the casserole dish with its cooking juices to the heat, bring to a boil, and reduce until a third of the liquid has evaporated. Stir in the shredded meat and fresh oregano. Remove from the heat.

Combine the melted butter and olive oil in a small bowl. Stack 3 circular sheets of yufka pastry and cut in half. Lay the halves on top of each other and cut into 4 equal wedges, so that you end up with 24 in total. Now cut off the rounded edges at the top of each wedge so that you have 24 triangles.

Brush some oil and butter onto one of the pastry triangles, spoon on some of the rabbit mixture and top with another pastry triangle. Seal down the edges, brush with some more oil and butter, then sprinkle with the extra za'atar (see overleaf). Repeat until you have 12 filled pastries.

To cook, brush a frying pan with the clarified butter and when medium hot, sauté the gözleme for about 1 minute on each side, until golden and crispy.

Makes 12

Swiss Chard Bulgur Pilaf with Caramelized Fennel and Za'atar

Most people wouldn't think of a pilaf as a snack, but it was in my house. I didn't eat a sandwich until I was about sixteen! A rice pilaf with spinach was always a favorite, but there were variations: purslane, Swiss chard, sometimes even dandelion greens. Pilafs are always best served with a dollop of chilled yogurt.

FOR THE CARAMELIZED FENNEL

- 1 medium fennel bulb, finely sliced
- 1 onion, finely sliced
- 3 tablespoons olive oil
- 1 tablespoon butter
- zest and juice of 1 small lemon

FOR THE PILAF

- 4 scallions, chopped
- 2 tablespoons olive oil
- 12oz/350g coarse bulgur
- 2 cups/500ml chicken or vegetable stock
- 14oz/400g Swiss chard leaves, chopped

TO MAKE THE CARAMELIZED FENNEL

In a pan, sauté the fennel and onion in the olive oil on low to medium heat for 10–15 minutes, stirring from time to time, until they are soft and caramelized. Remove from the heat and add the butter, lemon zest, and juice. Stir until the butter has melted, then put to one side.

TO MAKE THE PILAF

In a large heavy pan, sauté the scallions in the olive oil on medium heat for 3–4 minutes. Stir in the bulgur until the grains are well coated. Now pour in the stock, cover, and cook on low to medium heat for 15–20 minutes, until the bulgur is soft. A few minutes before the bulgur is cooked, add the Swiss chard and season to taste.

Serve the pilaf topped with the caramelized fennel.

For 8 to share

Saffron Yogurt Chicken
with Cumin Salt Aioli

8 chicken thighs, skin and bones removed

FOR THE MARINADE

1²/₃ cups/400ml plain yogurt

8 saffron threads

2 garlic cloves, crushed

1 teaspoon ground cumin

1in/3cm fresh ginger, peeled and finely grated

FOR THE AIOLI

½ teaspoon cumin seeds

¼ teaspoon sea salt

2 egg yolks

1 garlic clove, crushed

zest of 1 lemon

²/₃ cup/150ml light olive oil

1 DAY IN ADVANCE

Combine the marinade ingredients in a bowl. Add the chicken and coat well. Cover and refrigerate for a minimum of 4 hours, or preferably overnight.

TO COOK THE CHICKEN

Preheat a nonstick griddle pan or broiler to high and cook the chicken for 10–12 minutes on each side, until cooked through.

TO MAKE THE AIOLI

Place the cumin seeds and sea salt in a spice grinder (or use a mortar and pestle) and grind until almost powdered. Whisk the egg yolks (make sure you use top-quality fresh free-range eggs) in a bowl and add the garlic and lemon zest, whisking all the time. Drizzle in the olive oil until you have achieved the consistency of heavy cream (you may find that you don't use all the oil). Finally, stir in the cumin salt.

Serve the chicken hot, with the cumin salt aioli.

For 8 to share

Kadaifi-Wrapped Eggplant with Za'atar Rouille

Kadaifi pastry is like shredded filo pastry. It looks like a lot of loose strands and is generally used for wrapping sweet or savory fillings. Work fast because the pastry dries quickly—cover it with a damp cloth when you're not working it. Rouille is a Mediterranean sauce usually made with breadcrumbs. My twist on this classic is to use sweet potato.

FOR THE ROUILLE

- 1 large sweet potato, peeled and cubed
- 3 garlic cloves, chopped
- 1 green chili, seeded and roughly chopped
- 1in/2cm fresh ginger, peeled and roughly chopped
- 1 tablespoon za'atar
- juice of ½ lemon
- scant ½ cup/100ml olive oil

FOR THE EGGPLANTS

- 2 medium eggplants
- 7oz/200g kadaifi pastry
- vegetable oil, for deep-frying

TO MAKE THE ROUILLE

Cook the sweet potato in a pan of boiling water for about 20 minutes, until soft. Drain and allow to cool. Using a food processor, blend the garlic, chili, and ginger to a paste. Add the sweet potato, za'atar, and lemon juice, and season to taste. With the food processor running, slowly drizzle in the olive oil until you achieve a creamy, silky-smooth purée.

TO PREPARE THE EGGPLANTS

Slice the eggplants in half lengthways, then into ½in/1cm thick pieces crosswise. Lay some strands of kadaifi pastry on your work surface. Place a piece of eggplant at one end of the pastry and roll it up in the pastry. Repeat with the rest of the eggplant pieces.

TO COOK THE EGGPLANTS

Heat the vegetable oil in a deep-fryer to 350°F/180°C . Using heatproof tongs, place 2 wrapped eggplant pieces in the hot oil and cook for 2 minutes, until golden and crispy. Remove and place on paper towels to drain. Repeat until you have cooked all the eggplant pieces.

Serve hot, with the za'atar rouille.

For 8 to share

Langoustine Salad with Preserved Lemon and Za'atar Butter

FOR THE BUTTER

- 1 onion, sliced
- 2 garlic cloves, crushed
- 1 teaspoon olive oil
- 1 tablespoon za'atar
- 1 preserved lemon, skin only, finely chopped
- small bunch of fresh thyme, finely chopped
- 11 tablespoons/150g butter, softened

FOR THE LANGOUSTINES

- 16 large langoustines, shells removed
- 2 tablespoons olive oil
- generous pinch of sea salt
- ½ tablespoon sumac

FOR THE SALAD

- small bunch of fresh chives
- 12 red radishes, sliced paper-thin
- 1 red onion, peeled and sliced paper-thin
- 10 large green olives, pitted and roughly chopped

TO MAKE THE BUTTER

In a pan, sauté the onion and garlic in the olive oil on low heat for 5 minutes, until soft and mushy but not brown. Stir in the za'atar, preserved lemon, and thyme. Remove from the heat and allow to cool. Place the onion and garlic mixture in a bowl and work in the softened butter. Shape into a sausage, wrap in plastic wrap or parchment paper and refrigerate until needed.

TO COOK THE LANGOUSTINES

In a pan, sauté the langoustines in 2 tablespoons of olive oil on medium heat for 2–3 minutes. Season with the sea salt and sumac.

TO MAKE THE SALAD

Chop the chives into 1in/2cm slices, keeping the flowers intact. Combine the salad ingredients in a bowl. Spoon some onto each plate and top with a couple of langoustines. Melt a third of the preserved lemon and za'atar butter in a small pan and pour over the top of the langoustines. Serve immediately.

For 8 to share

Watermelon and Cherry Tomato Salad with Feta, Almond, and Za'atar Crumble

There is nothing that reminds me more of home than watermelons, great mountains of them piled up in the market. And there is nothing better than a heavily chilled watermelon slice on a hot summer afternoon. With this in mind, I created this salad. It's very simple and absolutely delicious. Make sure you use perfectly ripe watermelon and tomatoes.

FOR THE SALAD

½ medium watermelon, peeled and cut into chunky cubes

7oz/200g cherry tomatoes, halved

small bunch of fresh mint, leaves only

FOR THE CRUMBLE

7oz/200g feta cheese, crumbled

3½oz/100g almonds, lightly toasted and crushed

1 teaspoon za'atar

TO SERVE

fresh bread

white nasturtiums or if unavailable use herb flowers

Combine the salad ingredients in a large serving bowl. Mix together the crumble ingredients and sprinkle on top of the salad. Sprinkle with white nasturtium flowers. Serve with fresh bread.

For 8 to share

Duck and Black Sesame Za'atar Kleftiko

1 *large duck*

1 *tablespoon olive oil*

½ *teaspoon ground cinnamon*

2 *bay leaves*

4 *large potatoes, peeled and cubed*

2 *lemons, cut in wedges*

FOR THE ZA'ATAR

1 *tablespoon black sesame seeds*

½ *tablespoon sumac*

½ *tablespoon cumin seeds*

1 *small bunch lemon thyme, leaves only*

salt and pepper

TO SERVE

7oz/200g *fresh wild arugula leaves*

Preheat the oven to 325°F (275°F fan)/160°C (140°C fan).

For the za'atar, toast the sesame seeds lightly with the cumin seeds. Cool and grind in blender or with a mortar and pestle. Add sumac and lemon thyme leaves. Blend and season to taste.

Line a large baking tray with enough foil to make a sort of tent over the duck. Place the duck whole on the foil, season, and drizzle with the olive oil. Sprinkle on the za'atar and cinnamon, scatter over the bay leaves, and arrange the potatoes—all under the duck if possible, that way they cook best!—and lemon wedges around the base. Pull the foil over the duck, making sure it is sealed on all sides. Roast in the oven for 3½ hours.

When ready, take the tray out of the oven and carefully unfold the foil. Cook for 30 more minutes at 350°F/180°C. Cool and shred the meat, discarding bones and skin.

Serve the shredded duck with the warm potatoes and wild arugula leaves.

For 6 to share

Za'atar-Crumbed Shrimp and Sweet Potato Cakes

1lb/450g sweet potatoes, peeled and cubed

1 onion, finely chopped

½ teaspoon ground cumin

1 green chili, seeded and chopped

2 garlic cloves, crushed

5oz/150g raw jumbo shrimp, shelled and cut into small chunks

4 tablespoons olive oil

5 tablespoons breadcrumbs

small bunch of cilantro, finely chopped

flour for dusting

4 tablespoons za'atar

5 tablespoons breadcrumbs (extra)

5–6 tablespoons olive oil (extra)

TO SERVE

tahini, sumac, and lemon sauce (see p. 175)

Cook the sweet potatoes in boiling water for about 20 minutes, until soft. Drain and roughly mash, then season. In a pan, sauté the onion, cumin, chili, garlic, and shrimp in 4 tablespoons of olive oil on high heat, for 2–3 minutes. Remove from the heat and allow to cool for a few minutes in a mixing bowl. Add the sweet potato mash and fold in 5 tablespoons of breadcrumbs and the cilantro. Cover and refrigerate for 30 minutes.

The mixture will be quite sticky, so when you're ready, flour your hands and shape into 20 little balls, then pat them down into oval-shaped cakes. Combine the za'atar and the second 5 tablespoons of breadcrumbs in a shallow dish. Coat the cakes in the breadcrumb mix, then place on a separate plate ready to fry.

Heat the extra olive oil in a large pan and fry the cakes, a few at a time, on high heat. Place on paper towels to drain.

Serve hot with Tahini, Sumac, and Lemon Sauce.

Makes 20

Za'atar Crispy Fried Calamari
with a Spicy Walnut Cream

FOR THE CREAM

2 shallots, finely sliced

1 tablespoon olive oil

3½oz/100g fresh shelled walnuts

1 tablespoon fresh
breadcrumbs

1 tablespoon chili paste

1 teaspoon tomato paste

1 tablespoon pomegranate
molasses (see p. 175)

2 tablespoons olive oil (extra)

½ teaspoon hot paprika

FOR THE CALAMARI

2 large egg whites

1 medium-sized fresh squid,
approx. 1¾lb/800g

6 tablespoons flour

4 tablespoons za'atar

vegetable oil, for deep-frying

TO MAKE THE CREAM

In a small pan, sauté the shallots in 1 tablespoon of olive oil for 2–3 minutes on medium heat, until golden. Allow to cool slightly. In a food processor, blend the walnuts, breadcrumbs, chili paste, tomato paste, and molasses, until you have a smooth consistency. Add the cooked shallots and while still blending, drizzle in a little of the extra olive oil to achieve a thick creamy consistency. Finally, add the paprika, season to taste, and chill until needed.

TO PREPARE THE CALAMARI

Lightly beat the egg whites in a bowl. Slice the squid into ½in/1cm thick rings and drop into the egg whites, making sure the rings are well coated. In a separate bowl, combine the flour and za'atar, then drop in the egg-coated squid rings, making sure they are now well coated with the za'atar mixture.

TO COOK THE CALAMARI

Heat the vegetable oil in a deep fryer to 350°F/180°C. Carefully drop the squid rings, a few at a time, into the hot oil and cook for 1 minute, until golden brown. Remove with a slotted wooden spoon and place on paper towel to drain. It's best to avoid cooking too many rings at once, as it reduces the temperature of the oil and the calamari won't crisp up as well.

Serve hot, with the spicy walnut cream.

For 8 to share

Spiced Lamb Filo Cigars with Za'atar and Pistachio Cream

FOR THE LAMB

1	teaspoon olive oil
11oz/350g	lamb neck fillet, cubed
1in/3cm	fresh ginger, peeled and finely chopped
2	celery sticks, chopped
1	carrot, finely chopped
2	garlic cloves, crushed
2	green chilies, seeded and finely chopped
scant ½ cup/100ml	lamb stock
1	teaspoon ras-el-hanout (see p.182)
	salt and pepper

FOR THE CREAM

scant ½ cup/100ml	heavy whipping cream
1	teaspoon za'atar
2oz/50g	pack of fresh oregano, leaves only, finely chopped
1oz/25g	pistachios, finely ground
1oz/25g	pistachios, roughly chopped

FOR THE CIGARS

12–14	sheets of filo pastry
2	tablespoons melted clarified butter or ghee

TO COOK THE LAMB

Preheat the oven to 400°F (350°F fan)/200°C (180°C fan).

Heat the olive oil in an ovenproof casserole dish on the stovetop. Add the lamb whole and cook for 10 minutes, turning until brown on all sides. Add the ginger, celery, carrot, garlic, and chilies, and continue to sauté for 3–4 minutes before stirring in the stock. Cover and cook in the oven for about 45 minutes, until the lamb is tender and cooked. Remove from the oven and allow to cool.

Once cool enough to handle, shred the lamb into a bowl. Remove the vegetables from the casserole dish using a slotted spoon and add these to the lamb, mashing gently to combine with the meat. Sprinkle with ras-el-hanout, and season to taste.

TO MAKE THE CREAM

Whip the cream and add the za'atar, oregano, and both the ground and chopped pistachios. Combine well and season to taste.

TO MAKE THE FILO CIGARS

Cut the filo sheets roughly into 4 × 4in/10 × 10cm squares. Spoon some of the lamb filling along one side, not too near the edge. Roll once to seal in the filling. Fold in the sides, then continue to roll into a cigar shape. Use a little butter to seal the top edge down. Repeat with the remaining pastry sheets and filling. Arrange the cigars on a baking tray, seam side down. Brush with the remaining butter and bake in the oven for 10–20 minutes, until golden brown.

Serve hot with the whipped za'atar and pistachio cream.

For 8 to share

Turkey and Pine Nut Kebabs
with Saffron Mayonnaise

FOR THE MAYONNAISE

2 egg yolks

¾ cup/200ml light olive oil

1 tablespoon mild mustard paste

juice of 1 small lemon

4 saffron threads, soaked in 1 tablespoon of water

FOR THE KEBABS

14oz/400g ground turkey

3 garlic cloves, crushed

¼ teaspoon ground cardamom

1 teaspoon ground cumin

1in/3cm fresh ginger, peeled and grated

½ tablespoon chili paste

small bunch of cilantro, finely chopped

4 tablespoons pine nuts

TO MAKE THE MAYONNAISE

Whisk the egg yolks in a bowl, continuing to whisk as you gradually drizzle in the olive oil until you have a thick, smooth, and creamy mixture. Add the mustard, lemon juice, and saffron, combine and season to taste.

TO MAKE THE KEBABS

Combine the turkey in a bowl with the garlic, cardamom, cumin, ginger, chili paste, and coriander, and season to taste. Shape into 16 small oval patties, about 2in/5cm wide. Firmly roll them in the chopped pine nuts and cook under the broiler for 4–5 minutes on each side or longer, until cooked.

Serve hot, with the saffron mayonnaise.

For 8 to share

Orange and Za'atar Marinated Haloumi with Tomato and Za'atar Dressing

2 garlic cloves, crushed

2 tablespoons olive oil

1 tablespoon za'atar

zest and juice of 1 orange

11oz/300g haloumi cheese, cut into slices

FOR THE DRESSING

2 large ripe tomatoes, skinned and very finely chopped

3 tablespoons olive oil

1 shallot, grated

1 teaspoon runny honey

1 garlic clove, crushed

3 tablespoons white wine vinegar

1 tablespoon za'atar

TO SERVE

a few micro purple basil leaves

2 HOURS IN ADVANCE

Combine the garlic, olive oil, za'atar, and orange juice and zest. Place the haloumi in a bowl and cover with the mixture, making sure that the cheese is completely coated. Marinate in the fridge for at least 2 hours or overnight.

TO COOK THE HALOUMI

Using a heavy nonstick pan, fry the haloumi cubes on medium heat for 3 minutes on each side, until golden all over.

TO MAKE THE DRESSING

Simply combine all the ingredients in a bowl and season to taste. Drizzle over the hot haloumi, garnish with the micro-basil, and serve with fresh bread.

For 8 to share

Za'atar Red Mullet and Fennel Tzatziki Toasts

FOR THE TZATZIKI

- 1 large fennel bulb, trimmed and finely sliced
- 3 tablespoons olive oil
- 1 teaspoon fennel seeds
- 2 garlic cloves, crushed
- juice of 1 lemon
- 2¼ cups/500g thick yogurt or suzme (strained yogurt, p.182)

FOR THE MULLET

- 1lb/450g small red mullet fillets
- 3 tablespoons olive oil
- juice of 1 lemon
- 2 tablespoons za'atar

TO SERVE

- 8 small slices of chunky white bread or pita bread
- za'atar (extra, to sprinkle)

TO MAKE THE TZATZIKI

In a pan, sauté the fennel in the olive oil on low heat for 15–20 minutes, until creamy and caramelized. Remove from the heat and allow to cool. Meanwhile, toast the fennel seeds in a dry frying pan for 1 minute. Allow to cool, then finely grind the seeds using a mortar and pestle or a spice grinder. Combine the garlic, lemon juice, yogurt or suzme, and ground fennel seeds with the cooked fennel.

TO COOK THE MULLET

Brush the red mullet fillets with olive oil and cook in a hot, dry pan, skin side down first, for 3–4 minutes, until golden on both sides. Drizzle with the lemon juice and sprinkle with the za'atar. Season to taste.

TO SERVE

Toast the bread, then spoon some fennel tzatziki onto the toast, top with the red mullet, and sprinkle with za'atar.

For 8 to share

Lentil, Orzo, and Pine Nut Pilaf with Saffron Onions

9oz/250g dried brown lentils

5oz/125g dried orzo or long-grain rice

2 tablespoons olive oil

1 red onion, finely sliced

small bunch of fresh oregano, leaves only

3 tablespoons pine nuts, toasted

FOR THE ONIONS

2 onions, finely sliced

2 tablespoons olive oil

1 teaspoon saffron threads

TO COOK THE PILAF

In a pan, cover the lentils with cold water and cook on medium heat for about 20 minutes, or until the lentils are soft. Add the orzo and cook for a further 10 minutes, making sure the orzo is cooked through. Drain the liquid and keep the lentils and orzo warm. Heat the olive oil in a large frying pan, add the red onion, cooked lentils, and orzo, and season to taste. Stir and cook for 5–6 minutes. Remove from the heat, then add the oregano and pine nuts.

TO COOK THE ONIONS

In a frying pan, on medium heat, sauté the onions in the olive oil for about 15 minutes, until they are mushy and caramelized. Add the saffron and stir to combine.

Serve the pilaf hot, topped with the saffron onions.

For 8 to share

Chilled Carrot and Saffron Soup

1 onion, finely chopped

2 celery sticks, finely chopped

1lb/450g carrots, cubed

1 tablespoon olive oil

2–3 saffron threads

6 cups/1½ liters chicken stock

scant ½ cup/100ml coconut milk

2oz/50g pack of cilantro, finely chopped

In a large pan, sauté the onion, celery, and carrots in the olive oil on medium heat with the saffron for 5 minutes. Add the chicken stock, season to taste, and bring to a boil. Reduce to a simmer, cover, and cook for 15–20 minutes, until the carrots are soft. Remove from the heat and allow to cool, then blend in a food processor to a smooth purée. Return the soup to the pan, add the coconut milk, and simmer for 5 minutes. Allow to cool completely, then place in the refrigerator to chill.

Serve cold, sprinkled with coriander.

For 8 to share

Lemon Thyme Za'atar Fritto Misto

FOR THE LEMON THYME ZA'ATAR

8 *fresh oregano sprigs with flowers, if possible, roughly torn*

8 *fresh lemon thyme sprigs, roughly torn*

2 *tablespoons sesame seeds*

2 *teaspoons ground sumac*

½ *teaspoon salt*

FOR THE FRITTO MISTO

1 *small fresh squid, approx. 14oz/400g, cut into pieces*

11oz/300g *fresh jumbo shrimp, shelled, tails intact*

14oz/400g *small red mullet fillets*

3 *lemons, cut into ½in/1cm thick slices*

16 *lemon thyme sprigs*

2 *tablespoons cornstarch*

vegetable oil, for deep-frying

TO SERVE

4 *lemons, cut into wedges*

TO MAKE THE LEMON THYME ZA'ATAR

Simply combine all the ingredients in a bowl.

TO MAKE THE FRITTO MISTO

Put the squid, jumbo shrimp, and red mullet fillets into a large bowl along with the lemon slices and sprigs of lemon thyme. Sprinkle on two-thirds of the za'atar mixture, and gently toss to coat the seafood. Add the cornstarch and again, gently toss. Place batches in a sieve and shake to rid the mixture of excess cornstarch.

Heat the vegetable oil in a deep fryer to 350°F/180°C. In small batches, carefully drop the coated seafood and lemon slices into the hot oil. Cook each batch for 1 minute, until golden. Remove with a slotted spoon and place on paper towel to drain.

TO SERVE

Pile the seafood onto a large platter, serve with the lemon wedges, and sprinkle with the remaining za'atar.

For 8 to share

Fire & Noble Velvet

CHILI AND CUMIN

The **chilies** that are used in the Eastern Mediterranean are not as fiery or as furious as those that are used in some other cuisines. Instead they are fragrant, with strong aromatic tones. Used sparingly, they can add sweet, smoky, and nutty notes to a dish.

Aleppo, a town in the north of Syria, is famed throughout the region for its chili production. Green or red—my preference is red—Aleppo chilies have an astonishing depth of flavor that is reminiscent of dried fruits or flowers. They add a caramelized flavor to chili and za'atar chicken wings, and a sweet kick to cumin and chili-crusted calamari. If you can't get hold of Aleppo chili, which is usually sold as dried flakes, then use any mild and sweet variety of chili.

Cumin is a native of the Eastern Mediterranean, where it thrives in hot arid conditions. It has been used in the cuisines of Syria and Persia, modern-day Iran, for at least 4,000 years. The seeds can be used either whole or ground; it doesn't have the fire of chili but instead brings a whole labyrinth of elevating flavors, strong and warm, transforming dishes into something altogether more elegant.

The Greeks are so fond of cumin that they will keep a pot of ground cumin on the table to sprinkle on just about anything. It is great with meats, as part of a marinade, with pulses, or simply shaken onto breads and pastries before baking. Use fresh seeds whenever you can. Dry toast them, and then finely grind—that way you'll get the most out of the flavor.

Duck, Haloumi, and Green Chili Spring Rolls with Sweet Potato and Almond Skordalia

Skordalia is a Greek garlicky sauce or dip, usually made from either potatoes or bread. For a distinctive modern take on this traditional sauce I use sweet potato.

FOR THE SKORDALIA

- 1 large sweet potato, peeled and cubed
- 2 garlic cloves, crushed
- juice of 1 lemon
- 1 tablespoon ground almonds
- 5 tablespoons olive oil

FOR THE SPRING ROLLS

- 1 tablespoon olive oil
- 4 duck leg quarters, cut into small pieces
- ½ teaspoon ground cumin
- ½ small bunch fresh mint, chopped
- 2 garlic cloves, crushed
- 4 shallots, sliced
- 1 bay leaf
- scant ½ cup/100ml chicken stock
- small bunch of fresh parsley, chopped
- 7oz/200g haloumi cheese, crumbled
- 3 small green chilies, seeded and finely sliced
- 12 large sheets of filo pastry (8 × 8in/20 × 20cm)
- 5–6 tablespoons melted butter
- 1 tablespoon za'atar

TO SERVE

- 1 teaspoon za'atar

TO MAKE THE SKORDALIA

Cook the sweet potato in boiling water for 20 minutes until soft. Drain and mash in a bowl, then add the garlic, lemon, and ground almonds. While stirring, drizzle in the olive oil until well mixed, and season to taste.

TO MAKE THE SPRING ROLLS

Preheat the oven to 400°F (350°F fan)/200°C (180°C fan).

Heat the olive oil in an ovenproof dish. Add the duck quarters, cumin, mint, garlic, bay leaf, and shallots and cook for 5 minutes, until the meat is lightly browned. Add the stock, cover, and cook in the oven for 45 minutes to 1 hour, until the duck is tender and cooked through. Remove the duck and place to one side until it is cool enough to handle, then pull the meat off the bones and shred it into a bowl, discarding the skin and bones. Mix in the parsley, haloumi cheese, and green chilies. Add 6 tablespoons of the cooking juices.

Turn the oven up to 425°F (400°F fan)/220°C (200°C fan).

Place a large filo sheet on your work surface, brush with butter, then fold in two. Spoon some of the mixture in and gently spread along one edge. Fold in the sides to enclose the filling, then roll away from you to get a neat spring roll. Repeat the same with the remaining 11 filo sheets. Arrange the rolls on a baking tray seam side down, brush with the melted butter, and sprinkle with the za'atar. Bake in the oven for 5–6 minutes, until golden.

Serve the spring rolls hot with the sweet potato and almond skordalia, and sprinkle the skordalia with some za'atar.

Makes 12

Chili and Za'atar Chicken Wings

4 tablespoons olive oil

zest of 1 lemon

juice of ½ lemon

4 garlic cloves, crushed

1 tablespoon pomegranate molasses (see p.175)

2 tablespoons za'atar

2 teaspoons Aleppo pepper flakes

24 chicken wings

1 tablespoon sesame seeds, toasted

4 HOURS IN ADVANCE

Combine the olive oil, lemon zest and juice, garlic, pomegranate molasses, za'atar, and chili flakes in a large bowl. Add the chicken wings and make sure they are well coated with the marinade. Cover and refrigerate for 4 hours.

Preheat the oven to 425°F (400°F fan)/220°C (200°C fan).

Arrange the marinated chicken wings on a large baking tray lined with foil. Sprinkle with the sesame seeds and cook in the oven for 25–30 minutes, turning halfway through to ensure they're evenly cooked.

Remove from the oven and serve hot or cold.

For 8 to share

Carrot, Cumin, and Raisin Yogurt Salad

The Russians have vodka, the Japanese have sake, and the people of the Eastern
Mediterranean have raki. This mezze salad is the perfect accompaniment to raki,
or vice versa. Crunchy and creamy, it is reminiscent of coleslaw.

14oz/400g carrots, coarsely grated
1 tablespoon cumin seeds
2 tablespoons olive oil
1 cup/200g thick yogurt or suzme
(strained yogurt, see p. 182)
½ tablespoon mayonnaise
3 tablespoons raisins
2 garlic cloves, crushed

In a frying pan, sauté the grated carrots in the olive oil over medium heat
for 2 minutes, until wilted but not brown. Place in a bowl and allow to cool
completely. Roast the cumin seeds for 2 minutes, then cool and finely grind.
Once the carrot has cooled, add the yogurt or suzme, mayonnaise, raisins,
garlic, and ground cumin. Stir well and season to taste.

For 8 to share

Chili Chickpea Street Pilaf

One of the most common street foods in Turkey is a fluffy rice pilaf with chickpeas, known as nohutlu pilaf. It is claimed that this was one of the favorite dishes of the Conqueror, Sultan Mehmed II, and he ordered his chefs to add solid gold chickpeas to the real ones, so that his guests might share in the luck. I suggest that you use a can of chickpeas rather than solid gold, but this pilaf is still equally rich in flavor! The best rice to use is baldo, but Arborio or short-grain rice will work too.

1 onion, peeled and finely chopped

1 tablespoon clarified butter or ghee

9oz/250g baldo rice

7oz/200g canned chickpeas, drained

2 cups/500ml chicken or vegetable stock

¼ teaspoon chili flakes

½ teaspoon paprika

In a large pan, sauté the onion in the butter over medium heat for 2–3 minutes, until soft. Add the rice and stir well, ensuring all the rice grains are coated in the butter. Then add the chickpeas and stock. Cover the pan and cook on low to medium heat for 12–15 minutes, without stirring, until the stock is completely absorbed. The rice should be cooked but still have a little bite to it. Turn off the heat, cover the pan with a clean cloth, place a lid on top, and allow to rest for 15–20 minutes.

Serve with the chili flakes and paprika sprinkled on top.

For 8 to share

Quick Cumin Börek

My friend Sevda introduced this easy dish to me. A quick version of an old favorite, su börek, or water börek, is light, fast, and delicious. Yufka pastry is ideal for this recipe to work, as it's pre-cooked, but if you can't find it, use filo and add 10 minutes cooking in a preheated 350°F/180°C oven.

3 eggs, beaten
2oz/50g melted butter
scant ½ cup/100ml water
3 sheets of yufka pastry
9oz/250g feta cheese, crumbled
small bunch of fresh parsley, finely chopped
½ tablespoon cumin seeds

Combine the eggs, melted butter, and water, and season to taste. Cut the yufka pastry into small squares, approx. 1in/3cm, and mix the pieces into the egg mixture. In another bowl, mash the cheese with a fork and add the parsley and cumin seeds.

Heat a large nonstick pan over medium heat. Pour in half the egg and yufka mixture, sprinkle with the cheese, then finish by pouring on the remaining egg and yufka mixture. Cook on low heat for 3–4 minutes, until the underside is golden brown. Using a large plate, carefully turn out the börek and return it to the frying pan to cook on the other side for a further 2–3 minutes.

Enjoy hot or cold.

For 8 to share

Wild Garlic and Cumin Choux Balls

My mother used to make these with either spinach or fava bean purée. In this recipe I've substituted wild garlic for spinach, but you can use almost any green leaf vegetable. Another difference from my mother's recipe is that I use panko breadcrumbs. These are readily available in most Asian stores, but if you can't get hold of them, toast ordinary breadcrumbs so they have a crunch to them.

1 teaspoon olive oil

5oz/150g wild garlic leaves, trimmed and chopped

¾ cup/200ml milk

¾ cup/200ml water

7 tablespoons/100g butter

1½ cups/200g all-purpose flour

3 large eggs

5oz/125g feta cheese, crumbled

4–5 tablespoons panko breadcrumbs

1 teaspoon cumin seeds

vegetable oil, for deep-frying

TO SERVE

yogurt, mint, and garlic sauce (see p.179)

2 HOURS IN ADVANCE

Heat the olive oil in a pan over low heat. Add the wild garlic leaves and sauté for 2 minutes, then season to taste. Allow to cool sufficiently for you to handle. Squeeze out the excess water with your hands, then blend in a food processor to a purée and put to one side. Heat the milk, water, and butter in a small nonstick saucepan. Slowly bring to a simmer, making sure the butter is melted. Sprinkle in the flour, stirring as you do so. Continue to cook and stir for 3–5 minutes, so that the mixture starts to come away from the side of the pan. When the mixture forms a ball in the center of the pan, remove from the heat and, using a hand whisk if you have one or a fork if you don't, add the eggs one at a time, incorporating them into the mixture until it is soft and glossy. Now add the wild garlic purée and feta cheese, and mix again until well combined. Season and mix again. Place the mixture in a bowl, cover, and refrigerate for a couple of hours.

TO COOK THE CHOUX BALLS

Mix the panko breadcrumbs and cumin in a shallow dish. Shape the choux mixture into 20 small balls—about the size of golf balls—and roll each ball in the panko and cumin. Heat the vegetable oil in a deep fryer to 350°F/180°C. Drop the coated balls into the hot oil and fry for 3–4 minutes, until golden. When they float to the top, remove them with a slotted wooden spoon and drain on paper towel.

Serve with Yogurt, Mint, and Garlic Sauce.

Makes 20

Pumpkin Skordalia with Pine Nut and Nigella Seed Dukkah

FOR THE SKORDALIA

- 2 medium baking potatoes
- 1lb/450g pumpkin, peeled, seeded, and cubed
- 3 tablespoons olive oil
- 10 sage leaves
- 7oz/200g pine nuts, finely ground
- 4 garlic cloves, crushed
- 1 tablespoon lemon juice

FOR THE DUKKAH

- 3½oz/100g pine nuts
- 2 tablespoons dried coconut, grated
- 2 tablespoons coriander seeds
- 2 tablespoons cumin seeds
- 2 tablespoons nigella seeds
- ½ teaspoon salt
- ½ teaspoon crushed black pepper

TO SERVE

- small bowl of olive oil
- fresh crusty bread

1 HOUR IN ADVANCE

Preheat the oven to 400°F (350°F fan)/200°C (180°C fan) one hour in advance.

Place the baking potatoes in the oven and cook for 1–1½ hours (depending on size), until soft right through. Remove and allow to cool. Meanwhile, place the pumpkin cubes on a baking tray and drizzle with the olive oil. Season and sprinkle with the sage leaves. Roast for approximately 50 minutes, or until the pumpkin is well cooked. Set aside the oil.

TO PREPARE THE SKORDALIA

While the roasted pumpkin is still hot, place it in a food processor along with the cooking juices and sage leaves. Blend to a smooth purée. Scoop the cooked flesh from the baked potatoes and add it to the puréed pumpkin. Blend again, then add the ground pine nuts, garlic, lemon juice, and the olive oil in which you roasted the pumpkin. Blend until well combined. Season and place in a serving dish.

TO MAKE THE DUKKAH

In a dry frying pan, toast the pine nuts for 1–2 minutes, shaking the pan to toast evenly, until they are lightly golden in color. Turn out onto a board and roughly chop. Using the same pan, toast the coconut along with the coriander, cumin, and nigella seeds for 1–2 minutes, until you can smell the fragrant aroma. Remove and cool, then coarsely grind the mixture and combine in a serving bowl with the toasted pine nuts, salt, and black pepper.

TO SERVE

Serve the pumpkin skordalia and the dukkah in two separate bowls, accompanied by a small bowl of olive oil and plenty of crusty bread. Enjoy by dipping the bread in the oil, then into the dukkah, and finally topping with a generous helping of the pumpkin skordalia.

For 8 to share

Zucchini and Cumin Falafel

1 tablespoon olive oil

1 large onion, finely chopped

2 teaspoons ground cumin

¼ teaspoon ground allspice

1 cup/220ml milk

1 cup/100g chickpea flour

3 tablespoons canned chickpeas, drained

3 tablespoons lemon juice

4 small to medium zucchinis, grated and squeezed dry

vegetable oil, for deep-frying

2 HOURS IN ADVANCE

Heat 1 tablespoon of the olive oil and sauté the onion, cumin, and allspice for 3–4 minutes. Remove and transfer to a bowl.

In a medium nonstick pan, bring the milk to a boil then reduce to a simmer. Little by little, whisk in the chickpea flour until you have a smooth paste. Keep the mixture moving to avoid lumps. Season, then add the remaining olive oil and cook on low heat for 8 minutes, stirring all the time with a wooden spoon. Like choux pastry, the mixture will come away from the sides of the pan and work into a ball, solidifying as it is heated.

Cool the ball of paste, then mix in the sautéed onions, chickpeas, lemon juice, and grated zucchinis. Using your hands, mold the mixture into small balls and arrange on a tray. Chill in the fridge for a couple of hours.

TO COOK THE FALAFEL

Heat some oil in a pan, enough to cover the falafel balls, and heat until very hot. Carefully place the falafel, a few at a time, into the oil and cook for 3–4 minutes, until golden brown. Remove with a slotted spoon and place on paper towel to drain.

Delicious served hot with Carrot, Cumin, and Raisin Yogurt Salad (see p. 41), and Aleppo-Style Cumin Scented Baba Ganoush (see p. 56)

For 8 to share

Cumin and Chili-Crusted Calamari with Tahini and Chili Mayonnaise

FOR THE TAHINI AND CHILI MAYONNAISE

- 3 egg yolks
- 2/3 cup/150g peanut oil
- 2/3 cup/150g olive oil
- 1 tablespoon tahini
- juice of 1/2 lemon
- 1/2 tablespoon mild chili flakes

FOR THE CALAMARI

- 1 fresh medium-sized squid, approx. 1 3/4 lb/800g
- 4 tablespoons all-purpose flour
- 1 teaspoon mild chili flakes
- 1 tablespoon ground cumin
- 1/4 teaspoon salt
- 1/4 teaspoon pepper
- vegetable oil, for deep-frying

TO MAKE THE MAYONNAISE

Whisk the egg yolks and slowly drizzle in the oils, until you get a mayo-like consistency. Add tahini and lemon, and mix. Season and sprinkle with the chili flakes.

TO COOK THE CALAMARI

Slice the squid into 1/2in/1cm rings and dry with paper towel.

Combine the flour, chili flakes, cumin, salt, and pepper in a bowl and coat the squid rings in the mixture, a few at a time. Put to one side, ready to fry.

Heat the vegetable oil in a deep fryer to 350°F/180°C. Gently drop the coated squid rings, a few at a time, into the hot oil and cook for 1 minute, until golden brown. Remove with a slotted wooden spoon and place on paper towel to drain. It's best to avoid cooking too many rings at once, as it reduces the temperature of the oil and the calamari won't crisp up as well.

Serve hot, with the tahini and chili mayonnaise.

For 8 to share

Suzme and Chili Marinated Chicken Shawarma with Eggplant and Red Pepper Salad

8 chicken thighs

FOR THE MARINADE

3 tablespoons thick yogurt or suzme (strained yogurt, see p.182)

4 garlic cloves, crushed

6 tablespoons olive oil

zest and juice of 2 lemons

2 tablespoons white wine vinegar

2 tablespoons hot sauce

1 tablespoon Aleppo pepper flakes (or any mild red chili pepper flakes)

2 teaspoons cinnamon

1 teaspoon fresh nutmeg, grated

1 teaspoon ground cardamom

FOR THE SALAD

2 medium eggplants

3 red peppers

2 garlic cloves, crushed

1 ripe tomato, finely chopped

3 tablespoons olive oil

TO SERVE

2oz/50g walnuts, roughly chopped

2oz/50g pack of cilantro, finely sliced

TO MAKE THE MARINADE

Combine all the marinade ingredients in a bowl and season to taste. Add the chicken, stir to coat, and leave in a covered bowl in the fridge to marinate for 12 hours.

TO PREPARE THE SALAD

Preheat the oven to 425°F (400°F fan)/220°C (200°C fan).

Arrange the whole eggplants and peppers on an oven tray and roast for 20–30 minutes, turning so that all the skin is charred. Take out of the oven and allow to cool. Remove the skin from the eggplants and discard. Put the eggplant flesh in a food processor and blend until you have a smooth purée. Spoon into a separate bowl.

Remove the skin from the peppers, then seed and finely chop them. Add the chopped pepper to the eggplant purée along with the garlic, tomato, and olive oil. Season to taste.

Discarding the marinade, place the chicken under a hot grill for approx. 20–30 minutes until cooked right through, turning occasionally.

To serve, spoon the eggplant and pepper salad onto the plates and sprinkle with the walnuts and coriander. Shred the chicken, discarding the skin and bones, and layer on top of the salad. This is good hot or cold.

For 8 to share

Roast Pumpkin and Almond Soup
with Almond and Cumin Dukkah

Dukkah is an Egyptian spice and nut blend that has a fantastic crunchy texture. Here I've mixed the dukkah with olive oil so that it blends deliciously with this comforting autumnal soup.

FOR THE DUKKAH

2oz/50g whole almonds, toasted

1 tablespoon coriander seeds, toasted

½ tablespoon cumin seeds, toasted

¼ tablespoon fennel seeds, toasted

6 tablespoons olive oil

FOR THE SOUP

2lb/1kg pumpkin or squash, peeled, seeded, and cubed

8 fresh sage leaves, finely chopped

2 onions, quartered

6 garlic cloves

4 tablespoons olive oil

3⅓ cups/800ml chicken stock

3½oz/100g ground almonds

TO SERVE

3 tablespoons pomegranate seeds

TO MAKE THE DUKKAH

Place all the ingredients in a food processor and blend until well combined. Transfer to a small bowl.

TO MAKE THE SOUP

Preheat the oven to 400°F (350°F fan)/200°C (180°C fan).

Spread the pumpkin, sage, onions, and whole garlic cloves on a roasting tray and drizzle with the olive oil. Season to taste and cook in the oven for 30–35 minutes, until the pumpkin is soft. Remove from oven and allow to cool a little.

Using a food processor, blend to a purée, adding a little of the chicken stock to ease the process. Tip the pumpkin purée into a saucepan and add the rest of the stock. Simmer for 20 minutes, stirring from time to time to ensure a smooth consistency. Finally, add the ground almonds and combine well.

TO SERVE

Drizzle the soup with the almond dukkah and sprinkle with pomegranate seeds.

For 6 to share

Fava Bean and Green Chili Falafel with Yogurt and Tahini Sauce

Falafel plays a major role in every Eastern Mediterranean cuisine. Shaped into balls and deep-fried, it is made from dried fava beans or chickpeas, or a combination of both. Serve as a mezze dish with this yogurt and tahini sauce, or as an accompaniment to lamb or spinach dishes.

FOR THE SAUCE

scant ½ cup/100ml plain yogurt

2 tablespoons tahini

2 garlic cloves, crushed

juice of 1 lemon

¼ cup/50ml water

FOR THE FALAFEL

8oz/225g dried fava beans, soaked overnight

4 scallions, chopped

4 garlic cloves, crushed

small bunch of fresh parsley, chopped

small bunch of fresh mint, chopped

1 teaspoon cumin seeds, toasted and crushed

1 small green chili, seeded and finely chopped

1 teaspoon ground coriander

1½ teaspoons baking powder

vegetable oil, for deep-frying

TO SERVE

¼ teaspoon cracked black pepper

½ teaspoon sea salt flakes

TO MAKE THE SAUCE

Combine all the ingredients and season to taste.

TO MAKE THE FALAFEL

Drain the fava beans and place two-thirds of them in a saucepan with fresh cold water. Bring to a boil and simmer for 20 minutes, until tender. Drain and allow to cool slightly. Meanwhile, place the remaining uncooked beans in a food processor and blend until smooth, then remove them to a bowl. Put the cooked beans into the processor and blend to a purée, then spoon into a separate mixing bowl. Add the scallions, garlic, parsley, mint, cumin, green chili, coriander, and baking powder, and season. Finally, add the puréed uncooked beans to the mixture.

Shape the falafel mixture into walnut-sized balls and flatten into discs, about 1in/2cm thick. Heat the vegetable oil in a deep frying pan until very hot. Carefully cook 3 falafel at a time for 6–8 minutes, turning until evenly browned. Remove with a slotted wooden spoon and drain on paper towel.

TO SERVE

Arrange the warm falafel on a serving plate and drizzle over the yogurt and tahini sauce. Sprinkle with the black pepper and sea salt.

For 8 to share

Chicken Stuffed Yogurt and Cumin Pastry Börek

FOR THE PASTRY

2oz/50g yogurt

4 tablespoons/60g melted butter (plus 1½ tablespoons/20g extra, for brushing)

1 small egg, beaten

1 cup/165g self-rising flour

1 teaspoon cumin seeds

flour, for rolling

1 egg yolk, for brushing

FOR THE FILLING

2 shallots, finely chopped

1 small garlic clove, crushed

½ teaspoon ground cumin

¼ teaspoon paprika

¼ teaspoon chili flakes

1 skinless chicken breast, finely chopped

1 tablespoon olive oil

small bunch of fresh mint, finely chopped

1 HOUR IN ADVANCE

Combine the yogurt, melted butter, egg, flour, and cumin seeds in a bowl until you have a soft, pliable dough. Cover and rest in the fridge for 1 hour.

TO MAKE THE FILLING

In a nonstick pan, sauté the shallots, garlic, spices, and chicken in the olive oil on high heat for 3–5 minutes, until the chicken is well cooked. Remove from the heat and allow to cool, then add the mint and seasoning to taste.

Preheat the oven to 350°F (325°F fan)/180°C (160°C fan).

Place the dough on a floured surface and roll out to about 10 × 10in/25 × 25cm. Brush with a little of the extra melted butter and fold in half. Repeat this so that you have a small square. Brush once more, then cut the pastry in two and roll each piece on a floured surface to make 2 rectangles about 3mm thick. Split the filling between the pastry rectangles and spread along the length of the pastry, then fold each one over, sealing the edges and ends with a little water to make 2 sausages.

Arrange the böreks on a lightly oiled baking tray and brush with the egg yolk. Bake in the oven for 20–25 minutes, until golden brown.

Serve warm or cold, cut into bite-sized pieces.

For 8 to share

Lamb Moussaka Rolls

2 large eggplants

6 tablespoons olive oil, for brushing

FOR THE FILLING

1 small onion, finely chopped

1 tablespoon olive oil

14oz/400g ground lamb

2 large tomatoes, finely chopped

1 teaspoon ground cumin

½ teaspoon paprika

½ teaspoon mild chili powder

½ teaspoon oregano

small bunch of fresh parsley, leaves only, finely chopped

2 small tomatoes, thinly sliced

2oz/50g Parmesan cheese, grated

TO SERVE

1⅓ cup/300g thick yogurt or suzme (strained yogurt, see p.182)

1 teaspoon nigella seeds

TO COOK THE EGGPLANTS

Preheat the oven to 400°F (350°F fan)/200°C (180°C fan).

Thinly slice the eggplants lengthways, about ¼in/½cm in thickness. You should have 8–10 slices. Arrange the slices on a baking tray and brush generously with olive oil. Place in the oven and roast for 10 minutes, until soft and golden. Remove from the oven and allow to cool.

TO MAKE THE FILLING

In a large frying pan, sauté the onion in the olive oil for 2 minutes, until soft. Add the lamb and cook for a further 4–5 minutes, stirring to brown on all sides. Add the tomatoes, cumin, paprika, chili, and oregano, and season to taste. Simmer for 10 minutes, until any liquid has mostly evaporated and the mixture is thick. Remove from the heat, stir in the fresh parsley, and allow to cool.

TO MAKE THE ROLLS

Preheat the broiler.

Take a cooled slice of eggplant, place a spoonful of the filling on one end, and carefully roll it up. Arrange the eggplant rolls seam side down on a pan. Place a slice of tomato, or half a slice if that fits better, on top of each roll, and sprinkle with the Parmesan. Broil for about 2 minutes, until the cheese is golden.

TO SERVE

Place the yogurt or suzme in a bowl and sprinkle with the nigella seeds. Serve with the moussaka rolls, straight from the oven.

For 8 to share

Aleppo-Style Cumin Scented Baba Ghanoush

In Syria there are as many recipes for baba ghanoush as there are people making it.
Best made as they do in Aleppo, with plenty of cumin, or as they do in Damascus,
without cumin but with lots of fruity olive oil? More than one family has been
known to fall out over such matters. I prefer the Aleppo version, so here it is.

2 large eggplants

1 tablespoon ground cumin

1 small green pepper, seeded
    and finely chopped

1 small onion, finely chopped

1 ripe tomato, finely chopped

2 garlic cloves, crushed

    small bunch of fresh parsley,
    finely chopped

    juice of 1 lemon

2 tablespoons pomegranate
    molasses (see p.175)

2oz/50g walnuts, roughly chopped

Place the eggplants directly on a naked gas flame (or the electric ring if you
are using electric) and, taking care, cook on medium heat for 10–12 minutes,
turning occasionally, so that the eggplants are chargrilled evenly. The skin
will blacken and start blistering and the eggplants will become soft, not
to mention the fact that your kitchen will be filled with a wonderful smell.
Alternatively, you can bake the eggplants in the oven for 20 minutes at 425°F
(400°F fan)/220°C (200°C fan), but the flavor won't be quite the same. Once
cooked, place the eggplants in a strong plastic bag and allow them to sweat
for around 20 minutes, which will make them easier to peel.

Peel and chop the eggplants, discarding any uncooked pieces you might find.
Press the chopped flesh into a sieve. Over a bowl, press down gently to get
out as much liquid as possible. (Never be tempted to purée the eggplants.)
Discard the liquid. Tip the eggplant into a large bowl and, using a fork,
combine with the cumin, pepper, onion, tomato, garlic, parsley, and lemon
juice. Season to taste.

Serve drizzled with the pomegranate molasses and sprinkled with the
chopped walnuts.

For 6 to share

Sea Bass and Shrimp Mini Kebabs
with Tahini and Chili Sauce

FOR THE SAUCE

- 2 tablespoons tahini
- 1 tablespoon mild chili sauce
- zest and juice of 1 small lemon
- ½ large garlic clove, crushed
- 1 tablespoon olive oil
- 1 teaspoon sesame seeds, toasted
- ⅓ cup/80ml water

FOR THE KEBABS

- 2 sea bass fillets, approx. 1lb/450g each, skins removed
- 11oz/300g raw jumbo shrimp, shells and tails removed
- juice of 1 lemon
- small bunch of cilantro, finely chopped
- ¼ teaspoon ground cardamom
- 1 large red chili, seeded and finely chopped
- 2 egg yolks

TO MAKE THE SAUCE

Simply combine all the ingredients until you get a smooth sauce and season to taste. Add a little more water if needed to get a thinner sauce.

TO COOK THE KEBABS

Preheat the grill to medium/high.

Dice the sea bass very finely, until almost minced. Cube the prawns and mix together with the sea bass in a bowl. Add the lemon, coriander, cardamom and chili, then add the egg yolks. Mix well and season to taste. Using your hands, shape into small cocktail-sausage size kebabs. Grill for 3 minutes on each side, until golden.

Serve hot, with the tahini and chili sauce.

For 8 to share

Chickpea and Cumin Kofte with Tahini and Lemon Sauce

FOR THE KOFTE

7oz/200g dried chickpeas, soaked overnight

1 large onion, grated

1 ripe tomato, cubed

small bunch of fresh mint, leaves only, finely chopped

2 teaspoons ground cumin

1 tablespoon all-purpose flour (plus 3 tablespoons extra, for dusting)

2 tablespoons vegetable oil, for frying

FOR THE SAUCE

3 tablespoons tahini

juice of 1 small lemon

½ tablespoon sumac

3 tablespoons olive oil

scant ½ cup/100ml water

TO MAKE THE KOFTE

Drain the chickpeas and place in a saucepan. Cover with cold water and bring to a boil, then reduce to a simmer and cook for 1 hour or until soft. Drain again then place in a food processor, blending until you have a coarse purée.

Tip the chickpea purée into a bowl and add the onion, tomato, mint, and cumin. Season to taste and work in the tablespoon of flour until you have a pliable mixture. Using your hands, shape into small patties and dust with the extra flour.

Heat the vegetable oil in a nonstick pan and pan-fry the kofte, a few at a time, on medium to high heat for roughly 1 minute on each side, until golden. Remove and place on paper towel to drain.

TO MAKE THE SAUCE

Combine the tahini, lemon, and sumac in a bowl, adding 2 tablespoons of water at a time to thin the sauce a little. Finally, add the olive oil and sprinkle with sumac. Serve with the hot kofte.

For 8 to share

Spiced Pork and Cumin Sausages with Fennel and Preserved Lemon Salad

FOR THE SAUSAGES

1lb/450g ground pork

2 garlic cloves, crushed

1½ teaspoons ground cumin

¼ teaspoon ground nutmeg

¼ teaspoon ground cinnamon

½ teaspoon ground coriander

1 teaspoon mint

1 teaspoon oregano

½ teaspoon chili flakes

1 teaspoon paprika

scant ½ cup/100ml water

FOR THE SALAD

2 small fennel bulbs, sliced paper-thin

1 preserved lemon, pulp removed, rind finely sliced

10 green olives, chopped

small bunch of cilantro, finely chopped

3 tablespoons olive oil

3 tablespoons lemon juice

TO SERVE

3–4 tablespoons thick yogurt or suzme (strained yogurt, see p.182)

a few preserved green chilis

flatbread

TO MAKE THE SAUSAGES

Combine all the ingredients together, holding back some of the water until the mixture is moist but not too sticky. Season to taste, mix well, then using your hands shape into 16 small sausages. Cook at a high heat on a griddle pan or under the broiler for 3–5 minutes on each side, until golden and cooked all the way through.

TO MAKE THE SALAD

Mix together the fennel, preserved lemon rind, olives, and cilantro. Season to taste, then drizzle with the olive oil and lemon juice.

TO SERVE

Arrange the pork and cumin sausages on flatbread with the salad around it and a green chili and the yogurt or suzme drizzled on top.

Makes 16

Summer Squash, Feta, and Cumin Kofte with Wild Garlic Tzatziki

Tzatziki is normally made with cucumbers—this is a modern take on that theme.
If you can't get hold of wild garlic, then use watercress or spinach instead.

FOR THE TZATZIKI

11oz/300g wild garlic leaves, chopped

1 teaspoon olive oil

1¼ cups/300ml thick yogurt or suzme (strained yogurt, see p.182)

2 teaspoons olive oil (extra)

FOR THE KOFTE

1¾lb/800g summer squash, peeled and grated

5oz/150g wild garlic leaves, chopped

9oz/250g feta cheese, crumbled

4 scallions, finely chopped

2oz/50g pack of fresh thyme, leaves only, finely chopped

2 large eggs, beaten

1 teaspoon ground cumin

4 tablespoons breadcrumbs

3 tablespoons flour, for dusting

2–4 tablespoons olive oil, for frying

TO SERVE

1 tablespoon pine nuts, toasted

TO MAKE THE TZATZIKI

In a pan, sauté the chopped wild garlic leaves in the olive oil on medium heat for 1 minute. Place the sautéed garlic in a bowl and allow to cool completely. Once cool, combine with the yogurt and extra olive oil. Leave to chill in the refrigerator.

TO COOK THE KOFTE

In a large bowl, combine the squash, wild garlic, feta, onions, thyme, eggs, cumin, and breadcrumbs. Season to taste and refrigerate for 30 minutes. When ready to cook, shape into 25 small balls and dust with the flour.

Heat the olive oil in a nonstick pan and pan-fry the kofte on a medium to high heat for 5–6 minutes.

TO SERVE

Enjoy the kofte hot or cold, with the chilled tzatziki, sprinkled with toasted pine nuts.

Makes 25

Cumin Marinated Mackerel Fillets with Cumin and Lemon Thyme-Infused Shallot Purée

FOR THE MACKEREL

1 tablespoon ground cumin

4 tablespoons olive oil (plus extra, for brushing)

zest and juice of 1 lemon

12 small mackerel fillets

FOR THE PURÉE

16 shallots, sliced

1 teaspoon cumin seeds

1 tablespoon olive oil

scant ½ cup/100ml chicken stock

4 tablespoons heavy cream

2oz/50g pack of fresh lemon thyme, finely chopped

TO SERVE

1 teaspoon cumin seeds, toasted

1 teaspoon sumac

4 HOURS IN ADVANCE

Prepare the marinade by combining the cumin, olive oil, lemon juice, and zest in a bowl. Season to taste and add the mackerel fillets. Coat them well, then cover the bowl and leave to marinate in the fridge for at least 4 hours.

TO MAKE THE PURÉE

In a pan, sauté the shallots and cumin seeds in the olive oil on medium heat for about 8 minutes, until golden and soft. Add the chicken stock, turn the heat up a little, and cook until almost all the liquid has evaporated. Add the cream and simmer for a few minutes, again until almost all the liquid has evaporated. Allow to cool a little before seasoning and blending to a purée. Finally, stir in the lemon thyme.

TO COOK THE MACKEREL

Heat a griddle pan or heavy frying pan until it is very hot. Brush the mackerel fillets on both sides with olive oil and cook for 2 minutes on each side, skin side down first.

TO SERVE

Spoon some of the cumin and lemon thyme-infused shallot purée onto each plate and top with 2 mackerel fillets. Sprinkle with some cumin seeds and sumac and serve hot.

For 6 to share

Chili-Scented Shrimp and Feta Guvech

This dish brings memories of my father flooding back. Every weekend he would make one form of guvech or another. Vegetable guvech was his favorite and he kept an old earthenware pot for that sole purpose. Somewhere over the years the pot disappeared or was broken and now, whenever I am in Istanbul, I search through the bric-a-brac shops in the hope that I may find a similar one and thereby reproduce something even half as good as my father would make in his. Simple, but extremely tasty, you can also make this dish using haloumi cheese.

6 *scallions, cut into 1in/2cm pieces*

2 *garlic cloves*

1in/2cm *fresh ginger, peeled and grated*

½ *teaspoon Aleppo pepper flakes (or any mild chili pepper flakes)*

2 *ripe tomatoes, cubed*

1 *tablespoon pomegranate molasses (see p.175)*

3 *tablespoons olive oil*

½ *small bunch of oregano, finely chopped*

12 *jumbo shrimp, peeled and deveined*

2oz/60g *feta cheese, crumbled*

2 *tablespoons olive oil (extra)*

Preheat the oven to 425°F (400°F fan)/220°C (200°C fan).

In a medium-sized casserole dish, sauté the onions, ginger, garlic, chili, tomatoes, and pomegranate molasses in the olive oil on medium heat for 10 minutes. Stir in the oregano and season to taste.

Top the casserole with the shrimp and cover with the crumbled feta. Drizzle with the extra olive oil and cook in the oven for 10–12 minutes, until the cheese is golden and the shrimp are cooked through.

Delicious served simply with fresh crusty bread.

For 4 to share

Spicy Cumin Mussels with Pesto and Lemon-Infused Mascarpone

FOR THE MUSSELS

2lb/1kg *fresh mussels, scrubbed and beards removed*

3 *tablespoons olive oil*

2 *garlic cloves*

½ *teaspoon ground cumin*

¼ *teaspoon chili flakes*

1 *tomato, finely cubed*

scant ½ *cup/100ml dry white wine*

1²/₃ *cups/400ml chicken stock*

FOR THE MASCARPONE

11oz/300g *mascarpone cheese*

2 *tablespoons fresh pesto (see p.175)*

2 *tablespoons lemon juice*

zest of 1 lemon

3–4 *tablespoons olive oil*

TO SERVE

small bunch of fresh basil, leaves only

fresh, crusty bread

TO COOK THE MUSSELS

Ensure that the mussels are really well washed. Discard any that are already open. In a large saucepan heat the olive oil with the garlic, cumin, chili, and tomato. Stir for 1–2 minutes and when really hot, tip in the washed mussels. Add the wine and stock. Cover and cook for 5 minutes, shaking the pan from time to time. Take off the heat and discard any mussels that haven't opened.

Preheat the broiler to high.

Arrange the opened, cooked mussels on a deep, heatproof platter (one that will fit under your broiler) and save 4 tablespoons of the cooking liquid for the mascarpone.

TO PREPARE THE MASCARPONE

Tip all the ingredients, aside from the oil, into a bowl along with the 4 tablespoons of cooking liquid saved from the poached mussels. Stir thoroughly to combine, season to taste, then pour the mixture over the cooked mussels. Drizzle with the olive oil and place under the hot broiler for 2 minutes.

Serve hot, scattered with basil leaves and some fresh, crusty bread on the side to soak up the delicious juices.

For 8 to share

Cumin-Spiced Rabbit with Hazelnut Skordalia Sauce

FOR THE RABBIT

1 tablespoon ground allspice

½ teaspoon ground cloves

½ teaspoon ground black pepper

¼ teaspoon ground nutmeg

1 tablespoon ground cumin

2 × 2lb/1kg rabbits, jointed and cut into small pieces

4 tablespoons olive oil

2 bay leaves

2 cups/500ml chicken stock

FOR THE SKORDALIA

2 slices of white bread, crusts removed

3oz/80g ground hazelnuts

3oz/80g ground almonds

5 garlic cloves

¾ cup/200ml olive oil

juice of 1 lemon

¼–½ cup/50–100ml chicken stock (optional)

TO SERVE

5oz/150g Parmesan cheese, grated

TO COOK THE RABBIT

Preheat the oven to 400°F (350°F fan)/200°C (180°C fan).

Mix the 5 spices together in a bowl and add the rabbit pieces, making sure they are well coated. In a large casserole dish, heat the olive oil to high heat. Add the bay leaves and the coated rabbit pieces and cook for 5 minutes, until the rabbit is evenly browned. Add the chicken stock, cover, and place in the oven for 45–50 minutes, until the meat is tender. Remove from the oven and keep warm.

TO MAKE THE SKORDALIA

Soak the bread in a bowl of water for a few seconds. Squeeze dry and place in a food processor with the hazelnuts, almonds, and garlic. Blend while drizzling in the olive oil, until you have a smooth purée-like consistency. Add the lemon juice and season to taste. If you find that this is too thick a consistency for your liking, add ¼–½ cup/ 50–100ml of hot stock to thin a little.

Preheat the broiler to high.

Arrange the rabbit pieces in an ovenproof dish, spoon over the sauce and top with the grated cheese. Broil for a few minutes until very lightly browned, and serve immediately.

For 8 to share

Spiced Duck Rillette with Zucchini and Chili Pesto

FOR THE DUCK

⅔ cup/150ml thick yogurt or suzme (strained yogurt, see p.182)

4 tablespoons white wine vinegar

5 tablespoons olive oil

zest of 2 large oranges

½ teaspoon ground cardamom

2 teaspoons baharat (see p.173)

4 duck leg quarters

2 tablespoons olive oil (extra)

scant ½ cup/100ml water

FOR THE PESTO

2 medium zucchinis

1 tablespoon olive oil, for brushing

2 green chilies, seeded and finely chopped

2 tablespoons pine nuts, toasted and chopped

3 garlic cloves, crushed

1oz/30g Parmesan cheese, grated

15 basil leaves, finely chopped

3 tablespoons olive oil (extra)

TO SERVE

Turkish bread, or flatbread

1 DAY IN ADVANCE

Combine the yogurt or suzme, white wine vinegar, olive oil, orange zest, cardamom, and baharat in a large bowl. Add the duck legs, coat well, cover, and leave to marinate overnight in the fridge.

TO COOK THE DUCK

Preheat the oven to 400°F (350°F fan)/200°C (180°C fan).

Remove the duck legs from the marinade. In a nonstick, ovenproof pan, brown the duck legs in the extra olive oil on high heat for 5–6 minutes, turning halfway through. Add the water, cover with foil, and cook in the oven for 1 hour. Remove the foil and cook for a further 20 minutes.

TO MAKE THE PESTO

While the duck is cooking, preheat the broiler. Cut the zucchinis lengthways, in slices about ¼in/½cm thick. Lightly brush the slices with olive oil and broil for 1–2 minutes on each side, until golden. Allow to cool a little before finely chopping the cooked zucchini. Place in a bowl and combine with the chilies, pine nuts, garlic, Parmesan, basil, and olive oil. Season to taste.

TO SERVE

Once the duck has cooked, remove it from the oven and allow to cool enough to handle. Shred the meat and discard the skin (if you prefer). Gently toast the bread, lightly brushing with olive oil if you wish. Then place some warm sliced duck with a dollop of zucchini and green chili pesto on each flatbread.

For 8 to share

Cumin-Scented Jerusalem Artichoke Soup
with Fresh Crab

2 garlic cloves, crushed

1oz/30g butter

1 tablespoon olive oil

1lb/450g Jerusalem artichokes,
peeled and chopped

1 large potato, peeled and
cubed

1 tablespoon cumin seeds,
toasted

2 cups/500ml chicken stock
(vegetable stock may be used
as a substitute)

1¼ cups/300ml heavy cream

7oz/200g fresh white crabmeat,
cooked

TO SERVE

1 punnet of micro-basil (or
small bunch of fresh basil)

2 very ripe tomatoes, finely
cubed

In a large saucepan, sauté the garlic in the butter and olive oil for 1 minute on medium heat. Add the Jerusalem artichokes and potato and continue to cook, stirring all the time, for a further 5 minutes. Add the cumin and the stock and bring to a boil. Reduce to a simmer and cook for 10–15 minutes, until the artichokes are soft. Remove from the heat and allow to cool a little before blending to a purée in a food processor. Add the cream, return to the saucepan to warm through, and season to taste.

Serve in small bowls, topped with the cooked crabmeat and sprinkled with some micro-basil leaves and the cubed tomato.

For 8 to share

Spaghetti with Octopus and Aleppo Chili Sauce

1lb/450g octopus, poached (see p. 103)

3 shallots, finely chopped

3 tablespoons olive oil

2 garlic cloves, crushed

½ teaspoon Aleppo pepper flakes

⅔ cup/150ml dry white wine

6 large tomatoes, skinned and cubed

14oz/400g dried spaghetti

TO SERVE

small bunch of fresh oregano, leaves only

TO MAKE THE SAUCE

Remove and discard the octopus head, then slice the body and tentacles into 1in/2cm pieces. In a saucepan, gently sauté the shallots in the olive oil on low heat for 10 minutes, until soft and translucent. Stir in the garlic and chili, and season to taste. Finally, add the wine, tomatoes, and the octopus slices. Gently simmer on low heat for 20–25 minutes, until the octopus is very soft and tender.

Meanwhile, cook the spaghetti according to the package instructions.

TO SERVE

Toss the cooked spaghetti with the octopus sauce and garnish with the oregano.

For 8 to share

Cumin-Scented Chicken
Shawarma Caesar-style Salad

You might not think you know what shawarma is, but you do! Shawarma, or chevirme, comes from the Turkish meaning "turning," hence shawarma is the revolving meat on a vertical spit cooker seen in just about every Turkish restaurant and takeout place. Sliced and served with salad in a flatbread, shawarma is the best-loved fast food of the Eastern Mediterranean.

FOR THE CHICKEN

- 6 garlic cloves, crushed
- juice of 2 lemons
- 2 bay leaves
- 2 tablespoons ground cumin
- 1 teaspoon ground cardamom
- ¼ teaspoon ground cloves
- 1 cinnamon stick, broken
- ½ teaspoon mild chili powder
- 6 chicken breasts, skin removed

FOR THE DRESSING

- 4 tablespoons low-fat mayonnaise
- 2 garlic cloves, crushed
- 1 tablespoon tahini
- juice of 1 small lemon
- 3 tablespoons olive oil
- 3½oz/100g Parmesan cheese, finely grated

FOR THE SALAD

- 6 little gem lettuces, washed and broken into pieces

1 DAY IN ADVANCE

Combine the crushed garlic, lemon juice, bay leaves, cumin, cardamom, cloves, cinnamon, and chili in a large bowl. Season, then add the chicken breasts. Coat well, cover, and refrigerate overnight.

TO COOK THE CHICKEN

Remove the chicken from the marinade and cook on a griddle pan, or under a broiler, for about 15 minutes, turning to make sure it is evenly cooked all the way through. Once cooked, cut into slices.

TO MAKE THE SALAD

Combine all the dressing ingredients and toss with the leaves. Arrange the leaves topped with the chicken shawarma.

For 8 to share

Purple Citrus & Summer Breeze

SUMAC AND FRESH HERBS

I absolutely love the citrusy **sumac**. Whole, crushed, or ground, I don't care; it's my favorite friend in the kitchen. Sumac is made from the clusters of small crimson or purple berries from the bush of the same name. It is extremely popular in Turkish and Lebanese cuisine, where it is considered an absolute essential and is even used where others might add lemon juice or vinegar. Its versatility is phenomenal. It's fantastic simply rubbed onto kebabs and chicken; sprinkled on fish and vegetables; in sauces, marinades, and salads; to flavor butter; and to enhance the sweetness of tomatoes. Bright, lemony, fresh, and fragrant, it's enough to lift almost any dish.

What could be more redolent of summer than **fresh herbs**? My kitchen is filled with them, and the fragrance carried on a breezy day always evokes an Eastern Mediterranean summer's day. Parsley, mint, cilantro, and dill are the most commonly used herbs in Eastern Mediterranean cuisine. Buy them fresh or, better still, grow your own in pots on your windowsill and use them at every opportunity.

There is nothing quite as delicious and vibrant as parsley. There are two main varieties, curly and Italian flat-leaf. Personally, I prefer the flat-leaf, it being more fragrant and sweeter tasting than its cousin.

Fresh and fruity mint is found almost everywhere, and although there are more than a thousand different varieties, the best known are apple mint in herb salads, common garden spearmint with lamb, and of course peppermint to make a refreshing tea. Lemon balm is also of the mint family, and while more lemony than minty, it is equally refreshing.

Cilantro is another native of the Eastern Mediterranean, and every part is edible: the leaves, the root, and the seeds (coriander)—whole, crushed, or ground. If you grow your own cilantro in a pot, make sure that you only pick and use the young leaves. Older leaves can have an unpleasant, almost soapy taste.

Coriander seeds are warm, mild, and sweetly aromatic, almost citrusy, like orange peel. When ground they form an integral part of dukkah (a spice blend), but as they are very mild, you'll need to use a lot more than a pinch in a recipe to have any noticeable influence. Add to any chili dish, or combine with cumin as part of a falafel recipe.

The roots are full of flavor, so if you have a bunch of cilantro with the roots still on, cut them off, then wash and purée them with the leaves to give an extra zing to whatever you're cooking. It is particularly good for making a pesto, a traditional tarator, or a simple cilantro and onion whip.

Dill, with its delicate feathery leaves, has a very distinctive look. The taste, reminiscent of aniseed, can be overpowering, so use sparingly. It is best used fresh, as it loses much of its flavor when dried, and should, as a general rule, be added near to the end of the cooking process. It works really well with vegetables like fennel and fresh fava beans, and complements fish too, but don't go too crazy with it.

Sumac Tuna and Bulgur Tartare
with Wild Arugula and Fennel Salad

This is a light version of the traditional lamb kibbeh, which is a common street food all over the Eastern Mediterranean. There are hundreds of kibbeh recipes and almost every village has its own. Here I have substituted fresh tuna for the lamb. To serve the tartare you'll need a cutting ring.

FOR THE TARTARE

¾ cup/200ml water

⅓ cup/60g fine bulgur

11oz/300g fresh tuna, finely chopped

1 red onion, finely chopped

¼ teaspoon cayenne pepper

½ teaspoon sumac

¼ teaspoon ground chili

2 teaspoons small capers, well rinsed

FOR THE SALAD

5oz/150g wild arugula

1 small fennel bulb, finely sliced

4 pink radishes, finely sliced

3 tablespoons olive oil

4 tablespoons lemon juice

TO SERVE

½ teaspoon sumac

3–4 tablespoons olive oil

TO MAKE THE TARTARE

Boil the water in a pan, then drop in the bulgur and remove from the heat. Allow to stand for 8–10 minutes. Place the bulgur in a cloth and twist until squeezed dry, then put it in to a bowl. Mix in the tuna, red onion, cayenne pepper, sumac, chili, and capers. Season to taste.

TO MAKE THE SALAD

Toss the arugula, fennel, and radishes with the olive oil and lemon juice, and season to taste.

TO SERVE

Place a cutting ring in the middle of a serving plate. Fill with the tuna and bulgur tartare, smooth the top, and remove the ring. Top with a small handful of the wild arugula and fennel salad, sprinkle with sumac, and drizzle with olive oil.

For 6 to share

Zucchini and Dill Begindi

Hünkar Begindi means, depending on whom you ask, either "the Queen" or "the Sovereign" "was pleased" or "liked it." This dish was a favorite in the Ottoman Court, when it was made with eggplant and kashkaval, a mild, Cheddar-like cheese.

1¾lb/800g zucchinis, cubed

1 tablespoon/15g butter

2 teaspoons cornstarch

1–1¼ cups/250–300ml milk

3½oz/100g Gruyère cheese, grated

small bunch of fresh dill, finely chopped

TO SERVE

fresh crusty bread

Steam the zucchinis for 5 minutes, until soft. Remove and mash roughly with a fork. Put to one side and allow to cool. In a small pan, over medium heat, melt the butter. Stir in the cornstarch until you have a smooth consistency. Slowly add the milk, whisking at the same time, until you have a thick, smooth, lump-free sauce. If you want a thicker sauce, add less milk. Now stir in the grated cheese and remove from the heat.

Combine the sauce with the mashed zucchinis and sprinkle with the fresh dill. Serve hot, with fresh crusty bread.

For 8 to share

Sautéed Jumbo shrimp with Orange and Sumac Butter

This is as simple as it gets. The fresh, citrusy orange and sumac butter is the perfect partner to the delicate sweet jumbo shrimp. Try the butter with any grilled fish too.

FOR THE BUTTER

- 6 saffron threads
- ½ tablespoon ground sumac
- ¼ cup/50ml dry white wine
  zest and juice of ½ orange
- 7 tablespoons/100g butter, softened
- 4 garlic cloves, crushed
- 1 tablespoon fresh parsley leaves, finely chopped
- 1 teaspoon cumin seeds, finely ground

FOR THE PRAWNS

- 16 jumbo shrimp, shelled
- 1 tablespoon olive oil

TO MAKE THE BUTTER

Place the saffron and sumac in a small bowl with the dry white wine and leave to stand for a few minutes so that the saffron infuses. Now add the orange zest and juice. Combine this with the softened butter, garlic, parsley, and cumin, and season.

Shape the butter into a sausage shape, wrap in plastic wrap, and chill in the fridge until firm.

TO COOK THE PRAWNS

In a heavy pan, sauté the shrimp in a tablespoon of olive oil over medium to high heat for 2–3 minutes, stirring all the time. Add about 3oz/75g of the chilled orange and sumac butter to the pan, turn off the heat, and allow the butter to gently melt.

Transfer the shrimp to a warm serving plate and drizzle with the orange and sumac butter from the pan.

To serve, thinly slice the remaining chilled butter and place on the top of the shrimp. For a main dish, this is delicious accompanied by a simple green salad and some Jerusalem Artichoke and Tahini Hummus (see p.171).

For 8 to share

Haloumi, Walnut, and Frisee Lettuce Salad with Nigella Seed Vinaigrette

FOR THE VINAIGRETTE

- 1 tablespoon nigella seeds
- 1 tablespoon white wine vinegar
- 3 tablespoons olive oil
- 3 sprigs of fresh dill, finely chopped
- 1 garlic clove, crushed

FOR THE SALAD

- 1 large head of frisee lettuce, finely shredded lengthways
- 4 pears, quartered and finely sliced
- 3½oz/100g white grapes, halved
- 5oz/150g shelled walnuts, lightly toasted
- 3½oz/100g haloumi cheese, shaved as thinly as you can manage
- bunch of fresh chervil, leaves only

TO MAKE THE VINAIGRETTE

Whisk together all the ingredients, season, and put to one side.

TO MAKE THE SALAD

In a large bowl, gently toss together the lettuce, pears, grapes, and walnuts, and season to taste. Drizzle the vinaigrette over the salad and again gently toss to combine. Serve the salad in small bowls, garnished with the haloumi and chervil. The haloumi should be shaved so thin it's almost transparent.

For 8 to share

Caramelized Onion Salad with Sumac and Pomegranate Dressing

The combination of sumac and tomato was made in heaven. This salad is best in summer time when you can buy tomatoes that have not been grown in greenhouses, when they are sweet and delicious. I discovered this salad on my very first trip to Istanbul and I was blown away.

FOR THE SALAD

- 2 red onions, thinly sliced
- 2 tablespoons olive oil
- ½ teaspoon sugar
- 6 ripe plum tomatoes, cubed

FOR THE DRESSING

- 1 teaspoon ground sumac
- ½ teaspoon ground cumin
- 4 tablespoons olive oil
- 2 tablespoons pomegranate molasses (see p. 175)
- juice of ½ lemon

TO SERVE

- ½ pomegranate, seeds only
- small bunch of fresh parsley, chopped

TO PREPARE THE SALAD

In a frying pan, sauté the onions in the olive oil on medium heat for 10 minutes. Add the sugar and cook for a further 10 minutes, stirring from time to time until the onions are caramelized and soft. Remove from the heat and allow to cool completely.

Combine the tomatoes with the caramelized onions in a large bowl.

TO MAKE THE DRESSING

Combine all the ingredients and pour over the tomatoes and caramelized onions.

TO SERVE

Gently toss the salad and sprinkle with the pomegranate seeds and parsley.

For 6 to share

Chickpea, Sweet Potato, and Spinach Cakes with Creamed Parsnip and Cilantro Dip

FOR THE DIP

2 large parsnips, chopped

1 large garlic clove, crushed

juice of ½ lemon

3 tablespoons olive oil

small bunch of cilantro

¼ teaspoon coriander seeds

FOR THE CAKES

3 large sweet potatoes, cubed

14oz/400g canned chickpeas, drained

11oz/300g fresh spinach leaves, cooked

6 tablespoons breadcrumbs

1 teaspoon ground cumin

1 teaspoon ground coriander

½ teaspoon ground cardamom

all-purpose flour, for dusting

3–4 tablespoons olive oil

TO MAKE THE DIP

Cook the parsnips in boiling water for about 20 minutes, until soft. Drain, then purée in a food processor with the garlic, lemon juice, and olive oil. Season to taste, then stir in the cilantro and coriander seeds.

TO MAKE THE CAKES

Cook the sweet potatoes in boiling water for about 20 minutes, until soft. Drain and roughly mash. Add the chickpeas, spinach, breadcrumbs, and spices and combine well. Refrigerate for at least 30 minutes, then shape the mixture into 12 small patties and dust with the flour.

In a nonstick pan, heat the olive oil and pan-fry the spinach and potato cakes on medium/high heat for 2 minutes on each side, until golden.

Serve hot, with the parsnip and cilantro dip.

For 6 to share

Seared Scallops with Hazelnut Dukkah on Sumac Onions

FOR THE DUKKAH

3½oz/100g hazelnuts, blanched

1 tablespoon cumin seeds

2 tablespoons coriander seeds

2 tablespoons nigella seeds

1 tablespoon sesame seeds

2 tablespoons grated coconut
(here it is really good if
you can use fresh coconut
instead of dried)

FOR THE ONIONS

3 red onions, sliced

2 tablespoons olive oil

1 tablespoon pomegranate
molasses (see p.175)

1 teaspoon ground sumac

FOR THE SCALLOPS

12 large scallops

2 tablespoons olive oil

TO MAKE THE DUKKAH

In a dry, nonstick pan, toast the first five ingredients for 2 minutes on medium/high heat, stirring constantly. Add the coconut in the last 40 seconds. Transfer to a bowl and allow to cool completely.

Once cooled, place in a food processor, season, and blend to a coarse powder.

TO MAKE THE ONIONS

In a pan, on medium heat, sauté the onions in the olive oil for 8–10 minutes, until soft. Add the pomegranate molasses and cook for a further 2 minutes, by which time the onions will have started to caramelize. Stir in the sumac and remove from the heat.

TO COOK THE SCALLOPS

Brush the scallops with olive oil and fry in a hot pan for about 2 minutes on each side, depending on size, until lightly golden.

Spoon some sumac onions onto a large platter, top with the scallops, and sprinkle with the hazelnut dukkah.

For 8 to share

Cilantro and Onion Whip

This dip is the perfect accompaniment to grilled seafood and fish,
served simply with some fresh flatbread.

4 slices stale white bread,
  crusts removed

large bunch of cilantro,
  leaves only

1 red onion, chopped

1 free range egg yolk

scant ½ cup/100ml olive oil

TO SERVE

1 teaspoon ground sumac

Soak the bread in a bowl of cold water for 1 minute. Remove and squeeze dry. Place in a food processor along with the cilantro and onion and blend until smooth. Add the egg yolk and pulse again. Drizzle in the olive oil and season with salt and pepper.

TO SERVE

Place the cilantro and onion whip in a serving bowl and sprinkle with the sumac.

For 8 to share

Smoked Haddock and Sumac Whip

12oz/350g smoked haddock, skin and
  bones removed

2 tablespoons olive oil

juice of 1 lemon

small bunch of fresh
  oregano, leaves only, finely
  chopped

⅔ cup/150g thick yogurt or
  suzme (strained yogurt,
  see p. 182)

TO SERVE

1 teaspoon sumac

fresh crusty bread

Place the fish in a small saucepan and just cover with water. Bring to a boil, then turn down the heat and simmer for 2–3 minutes. Drain and discard the water. Allow the fish to cool enough to handle, then flake into a bowl and allow to cool completely.

Combine the flaked haddock with the olive oil, lemon juice, oregano, and yogurt or suzme, and season to taste.

Spoon into a serving bowl, sprinkle with sumac, and serve with some fresh crusty bread.

For 8 to share

Pistachio Dukkah-Crusted Duck
with Sumac Onion Jam

FOR THE JAM

4 *medium onions, thinly sliced*

1 *tablespoon/15g butter*

2 *teaspoons sugar*

1¼ *cups/300ml sherry*

1oz/30g *dried cherries, chopped*

1 *teaspoon sumac*

FOR THE DUKKAH

3½oz/100g *pistachios*

1 *tablespoon cumin seeds*

2 *tablespoons coriander seeds*

2 *tablespoons nigella seeds*

1 *tablespoon sesame seeds*

2 *tablespoons dried, shredded coconut*

FOR THE DUCK

4 *duck breasts, with skin*

1 *tablespoon olive oil*

TO MAKE THE JAM

In a pan, sauté the onions in the butter on medium heat for 8–10 minutes, stirring all the time. Add the sugar and continue cooking for a further 2 minutes. Now add the sherry and the cherries and reduce the heat to low. Cook for 45–50 minutes, or until the mixture becomes sticky and caramelized. Finally, stir in the sumac and season to taste. Put to one side to cool.

TO MAKE THE DUKKAH

In a dry, nonstick pan, toast all the dukkah ingredients for 2 minutes on high heat, stirring constantly. Remove to a bowl and cool. Once cooled, place in a food processor, season, and blend until you have a coarse powder.

TO COOK THE DUCK

Preheat the oven to 400°F (350°F fan)/200°C (180°C fan).

Rub all but 1 tablespoon of the dukkah powder over the duck breasts.

In a heavy, nonstick, ovenproof pan, sauté the duck in the olive oil on high heat for 2–3 minutes on each side. Now, with the skin side up, sprinkle on the remaining dukkah and transfer the pan to the oven. Roast for 12 minutes, then remove and leave to rest for 5–6 minutes before serving.

TO SERVE

Slice the pistachio dukkah-crusted duck. Spoon some of the sumac onion jam onto the middle of a serving plate and arrange the warm sliced duck on top.

For 8 to share

Wild Greens and Feta Börek

For this recipe you can use spinach or any seasonal wild greens that are available.

7oz/200g fresh wild watercress

11oz/300g fresh wild arugula

2 tablespoons olive oil

7oz/200g feta cheese, crumbled

½ teaspoon black pepper, crushed

½ teaspoon red pepper, crushed

2 eggs

1 cup/250ml milk

6 tablespoons melted unsalted butter

20 sheets of filo pastry

2 tablespoons nigella seeds

Preheat the oven to 425°F (400°F fan)/220°C (200°C fan).

In a pan, sauté the watercress and arugula in the olive oil for 2 minutes on medium heat, until just wilted. Once cool enough to handle, squeeze out the excess liquid. Place in a large bowl and combine with the feta cheese and the black and red pepper.

In a separate bowl beat the eggs, then stir in the milk and melted butter.

Lightly oil a 10 x 14in/25 × 35cm baking tray and lay in the first sheet of filo pastry. Brush generously with the egg mixture and top with another sheet. Repeat this until you have used 10 of the filo sheets.

Spoon on the wild greens and feta mixture and top with the remaining 10 filo sheets, brushing with the egg mixture between each sheet, as before. Pour any remaining egg mixture over the final layer and sprinkle with the nigella seeds.

Bake in the oven for 30–35 minutes, until golden brown. Remove and allow to cool before cutting into squares.

For 8 to share

Anchovy and Parsley-Stuffed Veal
Meatballs with Olive Oil and Garlic Cream

FOR THE CREAM

2 egg yolks

2/3 cup/150ml olive oil

juice of 1 lemon

1 garlic clove, crushed

FOR THE MEATBALLS

1lb/450g ground veal

1 egg

small bunch of fresh parsley, finely chopped

3½oz/100g Gruyère cheese, finely grated

2 hard-boiled eggs, finely chopped

3 anchovies, finely chopped

1 teaspoon ground cumin

3 tablespoons all-purpose flour, for dusting

4–5 tablespoons olive oil

TO MAKE THE CREAM

Place the egg yolks in a food processor and, with the setting on low, slowly drizzle in the olive oil until you have a smooth consistency. Stir in the lemon juice and garlic and season to taste. Transfer to a bowl and chill until needed.

TO PREPARE THE MEATBALLS

In a large bowl, combine the veal, raw egg, fresh parsley, and cheese. In a separate bowl, combine the hard-boiled eggs, anchovies, and cumin. Season and mix well.

TO ASSEMBLE THE MEATBALLS

Take a tablespoon of the veal mixture and shape it into a ball. Then, with a finger, make an indentation in the center and fill with the egg and anchovy mixture. Close up the meatball, ensuring the stuffing is fully enclosed, and roll it around in your hands before rolling in the flour. Repeat until the ingredients are used up.

In a nonstick pan, heat the olive oil and cook the meatballs, a few at a time, for 10 minutes on medium heat, until browned and evenly cooked.

Serve the meatballs hot, with the chilled olive oil and garlic cream, and Crispy Herb-Coated Zucchinis with Coriander and Lemon Confit Dressing (p.101), pictured pages 80–1.

For 8 to share

Fresh Crab and Cilantro Gözleme

11oz/300g fresh white crabmeat,
cooked

small bunch of cilantro,
leaves only, chopped

1 dessert apple, grated

juice of ½ lemon

2 large circular sheets of yufka
or filo pastry

4–5 tablespoons melted clarified
butter or ghee

Combine the cooked crabmeat, cilantro, grated apple, and lemon juice in a bowl and season to taste.

Lay 2 circular sheets of yufka on top of each other and cut in half. Lay the halves on top of each other and cut into 3 equal wedges, so that you end up with 12 in total. Now cut off the rounded edges at the top of each wedge so that you make triangles.

Working with one pastry triangle at a time, spoon some of the crab mixture into the middle and brush the edges with melted butter. Fold the points of the triangle so that they overlap and enclose the filling. Brush the tops with melted butter and arrange on a platter. Repeat until you have 12 filled pastries.

In a nonstick pan, sauté the gözleme in the remaining butter on medium heat for 2–3 minutes on each side, until golden and crispy. Serve hot or cold.

Makes 12

Gruyère and Mixed Herb Kadaifi Pies

5oz/150g Gruyère cheese, grated

3½oz/100g feta cheese, crumbled

½ small bunch of fresh oregano, leaves and flowers only, finely chopped

½ small bunch of fresh chives, finely chopped

½ small bunch of fresh mint, finely chopped

11 tablespoons/150g melted unsalted butter

14oz/400g kadaifi pastry

4 eggs

1¼ cups/300ml milk

1 tablespoon za'atar

TO SERVE

4–5 tablespoons runny honey

Preheat the oven to 400°F (350°F fan)/200°C (180°C fan).

Combine the Gruyère, feta, and fresh herbs in a bowl.

Brush 6 flat tart dishes, approximately 5in/12cm in diameter, generously with the melted butter. Take half of the kadaifi pastry and firmly push a layer of strands into the bottom of each dish, applying some pressure with the back of a spoon. Spoon the cheese and herb mixture evenly between the 6 dishes. Cover with the remaining kadaifi, again pressing the pastry down well. Generously brush each pie with melted butter. Keep pressing down to hold the unruly kadaifi pastry in place—you have to be quite forceful with the kadaifi. You may find that you don't need all the butter.

Beat the eggs together with the milk and za'atar, and season. Pour this onto each pie so that it soaks in.

Bake the pies for about 20 minutes, until they are golden and crispy.

Optional: drizzle with a little honey and serve hot. (No, you didn't misread it, honey—give it a try!)

Makes 6

Crispy Herb-Coated Zucchinis with Coriander and Lemon Confit Dressing

FOR THE LEMON CONFIT

2/3 cup/150ml water

3oz/80g sugar

1 lemon, finely sliced

FOR THE DRESSING

3 lemon confit slices (see above)

4 tablespoons olive oil

1 ripe tomato, skinned and finely chopped

small bunch of cilantro, finely chopped

FOR THE ZUCCHINIS

3 medium zucchinis

1 large egg

3 tablespoons panko breadcrumbs (or homemade breadcrumbs)

small bunch of fresh thyme, leaves only, finely chopped

small bunch of fresh parsley, finely chopped

vegetable oil, for deep-frying

TO MAKE THE CONFIT

In a small saucepan, slowly bring to a boil the water and sugar, stirring well to dissolve the sugar. Reduce to a simmer and continue to stir for about 3 minutes, until you have a thick syrup. Add the lemon slices and cook on low heat for 10 minutes, until they are translucent. Drain the lemon slices and discard the syrup. The lemon confit slices you don't use in this recipe will keep for a week.

TO MAKE THE DRESSING

Finely chop 3 of the lemon confit slices and place them in a bowl with the olive oil, tomato, and cilantro. Mix well and season to taste.

TO PREPARE THE ZUCCHINIS

Slice the zucchinis into 1–1½in/3–4cm chunky strips. In a bowl, beat the egg and add the zucchini. In a separate bowl, combine the panko breadcrumbs with the fresh herbs. Drop the egg-coated zucchinis into the breadcrumbs and herbs and coat well.

Heat the vegetable oil in a deep fryer to 350°F/180°C. Carefully drop a few zucchini discs into the oil and cook for 2–3 minutes, until golden. Remove with a slotted wooden spoon and drain on paper towel. Repeat until all the zucchini discs are cooked.

Serve the crispy zucchinis hot, with the lemon confit dressing on the side to dip.

For 8 to share

Sumac Octopus with Pomegranate

Octopus can be very tough, so it is best poached before using it in a dish.
Use fresh octopus if possible; if using frozen, be sure to defrost thoroughly.

4 cups/1 liter water

3 tablespoons white wine
    vinegar

juice of ½ lemon

2 bay leaves

3 black peppercorns

½ tablespoon sea salt

1 whole octopus, approx.
    3lb/1½ kg

4 tablespoons white wine
    vinegar

2 tablespoons pomegranate
    molasses (see p. 175)

1 tablespoon superfine sugar

½ tablespoon ground sumac

1 red onion, finely sliced

TO SERVE

3–4 tablespoons olive oil

1 pomegranate, seeds only

small bunch of fresh
    oregano, leaves only, finely
    chopped

ground sumac (extra)

fresh bread

TO POACH THE OCTOPUS

Boil 4 cups/1 liter of water in a saucepan and add the white wine vinegar, lemon juice, bay leaves, black peppercorns, and sea salt. Reduce the heat and simmer for 10 minutes. Using tongs and holding the octopus by the head, dip it in the simmering poaching liquid 3 times, for about 15 seconds each time. This is known as scaring and will prevent the octopus tentacles curling up.

Next, place the octopus in the simmering water and allow to cook for 30–40 minutes. Drain and cool then remove the head and use just the body and tentacles. This method of cooking the octopus is the same whether you are going to grill it afterwards or just marinate it as here.

In a bowl, combine the white wine vinegar, pomegranate molasses, sugar, and sumac. Stir until the sugar is completely dissolved. Season, then add the red onion and chill in the fridge for 30 minutes.

TO SERVE

Slice the octopus very thinly, almost sashimi style, and arrange on a platter. Pour over the pomegranate mixture, then drizzle with the olive oil. Scatter over the pomegranate seeds and oregano leaves. Season to taste and finally sprinkle with the extra sumac. Serve with fresh bread.

For 8 to share

Lentil and Parsley Tabbouleh with
Wild Garlic and Sesame Suzme

FOR THE TABBOULEH

2oz/50g *Puy lentils*

bunch of fresh parsley, leaves only, finely chopped

1 *large ripe tomato, skinned and finely chopped*

2 *shallots, finely chopped*

juice of 1 lemon

2 *tablespoons olive oil*

1 *teaspoon sumac*

FOR THE SUZME

scant 1 *tablespoon/10g butter*

7oz/200g *wild garlic, leaves only (substitute with spinach if you can't get wild garlic)*

14oz/400g *thick yogurt or suzme (strained yogurt, see p. 182)*

1 *tablespoon black sesame seeds*

TO PREPARE THE TABBOULEH

Bring a large saucepan of water to a boil and cook the lentils according to the package instructions, for around 20 minutes, until soft. Drain, put into a bowl, and allow to cool. Once the lentils have cooled, combine with the parsley, tomato, shallots, lemon juice, olive oil, and sumac.

TO MAKE THE SUZME

In a large saucepan, melt the butter and sauté the wild garlic leaves for 2–3 minutes, until just wilted. Season to taste and leave to cool completely. Once cooled, mix with the suzme and the sesame seeds.

Serve the lentil tabbouleh accompanied by the wild garlic and sesame suzme.

For 8 to share

Skordalia Cavolo Nero Cakes topped with Shredded Duck Confit and Pomegranate

Cavolo nero is a strong-flavored Italian kale with dark green leaves, also known as Tuscan kale, black cabbage, lacinato, and dinosaur kale. Confit is any meat slowly cooked in fat and it really is worth using. Duck confit can be bought in cans, or you can make it yourself. Alternatively, use conventionally roasted duck legs.

FOR THE CAKES

2	large baking potatoes
7oz/200g	cavolo nero, chopped into small pieces
	bunch of fresh basil, chopped
2	garlic cloves, crushed
5	tablespoons ground almonds
6	tablespoons olive oil
1	tablespoon lemon juice
4–5	tablespoons panko breadcrumbs
2	tablespoons olive oil (extra)

FOR THE DUCK

4	duck confit quarters
2	teaspoons pomegranate molasses (see p. 175)
1	pomegranate, seeds only

TO COOK THE CAKES

Preheat the oven to 400°F (350°F fan)/200°C (180°C fan).

Bake the potatoes in the oven for at least an hour, until the insides are soft. Let them cool, then scoop out the insides, discarding the skins. Mash the potato into a smooth purée, and season to taste.

Place the cavolo nero in a small saucepan, cover with water, and bring to a boil. Reduce to a simmer and cook for 3 minutes, until soft. Drain and stir into the mashed potatoes along with the basil, garlic, ground almonds, olive oil, and lemon juice. Combine well, or if preferred blend in a food processor to a smooth purée, and season to taste. Shape into golfball-sized cakes and flatten slightly.

Coat the cakes in the panko breadcrumbs and lightly fry them, a few at a time, in the extra olive oil on medium heat for 2–3 minutes, until golden brown. Remove and arrange on a platter.

TO PREPARE THE DUCK

Shred the duck confit into small pieces with your fingers, discarding the skin and bones, and place in a bowl. Add the molasses and pomegranate seeds, stir to coat well, and season to taste.

Serve the skordalia cakes hot or cold, with the duck generously piled on top.

For 8 to share

Sumac and Pistachio Dukkah
Shrimp with Tahini Sauce

FOR THE DUKKAH

4 tablespoons black sesame
  seeds

3 tablespoons cumin seeds

3 tablespoons pistachios

1 teaspoon sea salt

1 teaspoon ground sumac

FOR THE SAUCE

¼ cup/50ml tahini

1 garlic clove, crushed

½ tablespoon ground cumin

3 tablespoons olive oil

  juice of 1 lemon

scant ½ cup/100ml cold water

FOR THE SHRIMP

1 tablespoon olive oil

16 jumbo shrimp, peeled and
  deveined

TO SERVE

nasturtium flowers

fresh flatbread

TO MAKE THE DUKKAH

In a dry frying pan, toast the sesame seeds, cumin seeds, and pistachios on high heat for 1 minute. Remove and allow to cool before roughly grinding them with the sea salt and sumac.

TO MAKE THE SAUCE

Combine all the ingredients, adding the lemon juice last, and season to taste. The consistency should be like heavy cream, so add a little more cold water to further thin it, if required.

TO COOK THE PRAWNS

In a nonstick pan, heat the olive oil and cook the shrimp for 3–4 minutes on medium heat, until lightly golden. Remove from the pan using a slotted wooden spoon and arrange on a platter. Drizzle with the tahini sauce, sprinkle with the dukkah, then scatter the nasturtium flowers around.

A simple yet stunning sharing dish best accompanied simply with some fresh flatbread.

For 8 to share

Crushed Fava Beans and Avocado
with Parmesan and Sumac Biscuits

FOR THE BISCUITS

5oz/125g Parmesan, grated

10 tablespoons/125g butter, cubed

scant 1 cup/125g all-purpose flour (and extra for dusting)

½ tablespoon ground sumac

5–6 tablespoons melted butter, for brushing

1 tablespoon black sesame seeds

FOR THE BEANS

2lb/1kg fresh or frozen fava (broad) beans, shelled

1 ripe avocado

juice of 1 small lemon

2 tablespoons olive oil

1 tablespoon tahini

½ teaspoon ground sumac

TO MAKE THE BISCUITS

Preheat the oven to 400°F (350°F fan)/200°C (180°C fan).

Place the Parmesan, cubed butter, flour, and sumac in a food processor and blend until well combined. Tip onto a flour-dusted surface and work into a smooth dough. Separate into 4 equal pieces, roll each to about ¼in/½cm thickness between parchment paper, lift the top parchment off, then brush with a little melted butter and sprinkle with sesame seeds.

Arrange the dough on a baking tray and cook for 8 minutes, until just golden. Remove and cool slightly before breaking each piece into 4–5 smaller biscuits.

TO PREPARE THE BEANS

Heat a large saucepan of water, add the fava beans, and boil for 10 minutes. Immediately drain and rinse under cold water. Peel the skins off the beans and discard.

In a food processor, briefly blend the beans with the avocado, lemon juice, olive oil, tahini, and sumac, so that the beans are still a little chunky.

Season to taste and serve with the Parmesan and sumac biscuits.

For 8 to share

Sumac-Crusted Tuna
with Pink Grapefruit Salsa

FOR THE SALSA

2 pink grapefruits, peeled and
  finely chopped

2 blood oranges, peeled and
  finely chopped

  small bunch of fresh parsley,
  finely chopped

1 red onion, finely sliced

  juice of 1 small lemon

1 teaspoon ground sumac

FOR THE TUNA

2 tablespoons ground sumac

1 teaspoon ground cumin

½ teaspoon ground black
  pepper

14oz/400g tuna steaks, cut into long
  strips

2 tablespoons olive oil

TO MAKE THE SALSA

Combine the grapefruit, orange, parsley, and red onion in a bowl. Toss with the lemon juice, add the crushed sumac, and season to taste. Set aside.

TO COOK THE TUNA

Preheat the broiler.

In a separate bowl, mix the sumac, cumin, and black pepper. Brush the strips of tuna with the olive oil, then coat with the spice mix. Broil the tuna for 2–3 minutes on each side.

Serve hot, with the grapefruit salsa.

For 8 to share

Cardamom Duck with Orange and Sumac Infused Sauce

This is so easy to prepare and a real crowd-pleaser. Serve with a rice pilaf.

4 *large duck breasts, with skin*

FOR THE SAUCE

4 *shallots, finely chopped*

¼ *teaspoon cardamom seeds, lightly crushed*

¾ *cup/200ml chicken stock*
   juice of 1 large orange

1 *teaspoon ground sumac*

1½ *tablespoons/20g butter*

TO COOK THE DUCK

Score the skin of the duck breasts and season with salt and pepper. Heat a heavy pan over low to medium heat and sear the duck breasts on both sides for 10 minutes, until browned. Increase the heat to high and cook skin side down for 2 more minutes, until the skin is crisp. Remove the duck from the pan and set aside to rest in a warm place. Leave any juices and fat in the pan.

TO MAKE THE SAUCE

Keep the high heat under the pan in which you cooked the duck and sauté the shallots for 5 minutes. Add the cardamom seeds and stir for a minute longer. Skim off the excess fat and add the stock and orange juice. Season to taste and simmer for 8–10 minutes, until the liquid has reduced by half. Add the sumac, stir to combine, and remove from the heat.

Strain the sauce through a sieve and discard any solids. Finally, whisk in the butter.

Slice the duck and pour over the sauce. Serve with Lentil, Orzo, and Pinenut Pilaf with Saffron Onions (see p.32)

For 8 to share

Potato Gnocchi with Coconut and Mascarpone Sauce and Coriander Coconut Dukkah

For this, use fresh coconut for the best flavor although dried, shredded coconut can be substituted if more convenient.

FOR THE GNOCCHI

1lb/450g starchy potatoes, such as russets

1 egg yolk

pinch of salt

1 cup/150g all-purpose flour

FOR THE SAUCE

4 tablespoons coconut milk

5oz/150g mascarpone cheese

1½oz/40g fresh coconut, grated

½ small bunch of cilantro, finely chopped

FOR THE DUKKAH

3½oz/100g blanched almonds

2 tablespoons coriander seeds

2 tablespoons cumin seeds

2 tablespoons grated fresh coconut

2 tablespoons sesame seeds

½ teaspoon salt

½ teaspoon black pepper

TO SERVE

nasturtium flowers, to serve

TO MAKE THE GNOCCHI

Preheat the oven to 425°F (400°F fan)/220°C (200°C fan). Bake the potatoes for 1½ hours. Remove from the oven and leave until cool enough to handle. Halve the potatoes and scoop out the flesh into a bowl. Put the potato flesh through a potato ricer, to mash finely. Add the egg yolk, salt, and three-quarters of the flour, mixing well to form a smooth dough, adding the remaining flour if required.

Divide the dough into 4 pieces, then roll into sausage shapes, about 1in/2½cm thick. Cut the sausages into ½in/1cm long pieces and arrange on a floured tray. Gently press each of the gnocchi with a fork to flatten slightly.

Boil a saucepan of water and drop in the gnocchi. Cook for 2–3 minutes, until they rise to the surface of the water, then drain immediately.

TO MAKE THE SAUCE

In a small pan, cook the coconut milk and mascarpone on medium heat for 3–4 minutes. Season to taste and stir in the grated coconut and cilantro.

TO MAKE THE DUKKAH

Place all the ingredients in a hot, dry frying pan and gently toast for 2 minutes, stirring all the time. Cool and grind roughly with a mortar and pestle.

Add the cooked gnocchi to the coconut and mascarpone sauce and coat well. Serve sprinkled with the coriander coconut dukkah, and decorate with a few nasturtium petals.

For 8 to share

White Bean, Parsley, and Caramelized Fennel Salad with Lemon and Tahini Dressing

This is my version of a *piyaz*, a name that is generally given to all bean salads. In Persian, the word means onion, which is also a common ingredient. *Piyaz* can be either eaten as a main course or as a salad to accompany kofte. I have used dried beans in this recipe but you can use canned beans to speed things up.

FOR THE SALAD

- 3 tablespoons olive oil
- 1 medium fennel bulb, thinly sliced
- 1 onion, thinly sliced
- scant 1 tablespoon/10g butter
- zest and juice of 1 small lemon
- 12oz/350g dried navy beans, soaked overnight
- small bunch of fresh parsley, finely chopped
- ½ teaspoon sumac

FOR THE DRESSING

- 2 tablespoons tahini
- zest and juice of 1 small lemon
- ½ garlic clove
- 1 tablespoon olive oil
- ⅓ cup water

TO PREPARE THE SALAD

Heat the oil in a saucepan and sauté the fennel and onion over low heat for 10–15 minutes, stirring from time to time, until they are soft and caramelized. Season to taste and remove from the heat before stirring in the butter, lemon zest, and lemon juice. Put to one side to cool.

Drain the soaked beans and place in a large saucepan. Cover with cold water and bring to a boil. Reduce to a simmer and cook for 25–30 minutes, until the beans are soft. Drain, then put the beans into a large serving bowl. Allow to cool, then add the caramelized fennel and onion, parsley, and sumac. Combine well and season to taste.

TO MAKE THE DRESSING

Combine all the dressing ingredients in a separate bowl, adding more water if needed to get a thinner dressing consistency, then drizzle over the salad and serve.

For 8 to share

Veal and Pistachio Mini Burgers with Fried Sumac Onions

FOR THE ONIONS

2 teaspoons olive oil

1 large onion, thinly sliced

1 teaspoon ground sumac

FOR THE BURGERS

2lb/950g veal, finely chopped

2 large eggs

2in/5cm fresh ginger, peeled and finely grated

2 green chilies, seeded and finely chopped

1 teaspoon ground cumin

1 onion, grated

4oz/120g pistachios, skinless, chopped

TO SERVE

4 Turkish pita bread or 1 large focaccia loaf

20 sprigs parsley

tahini mayonnaise (see p.179)

TO COOK THE ONION

Heat the olive oil in a frying pan over a low to medium heat, then add the sliced onion and sauté until golden. Sprinkle with the sumac and remove from the heat.

TO MAKE THE BURGERS

Preheat the grill or broiler to medium/high.

Mix the veal in a bowl with the eggs, ginger, chilies, cumin, onion, and pistachios. Knead to combine really well, then shape the mixture into 16 small burgers.

Grill or broil the burgers for at least 3 minutes on each side, until golden and cooked right through.

TO SERVE

Make the burger rolls by cutting burger shapes from pita bread or the focaccia, using a small, round pastry cutter. Top half a toasted burger bun with a veal and pistachio burger and a helping of fried sumac onions, adding a sprig of flat parsley and a spoonful of Tahini Mayonnaise. Cover with the remaining half bun and serve.

Makes 16

Fava Bean, Wild Garlic, and Fennel Dip

Fava beans are a much-loved ingredient in Eastern Mediterranean cuisine.
This recipe is based on a classic Turkish dip, and is best made with fresh beans
for a creamier consistency. Either way, always remove the hard outer skins
of the fava beans once they are cooked. If you can't find fresh fava beans
then use frozen.

11oz/300g	fresh fava (broad) beans, shelled (approx. 2lb/1kg unshelled)
2	tablespoons olive oil
1	medium fennel bulb, finely sliced
2	shallots, finely sliced
½	teaspoon brown sugar
11oz/300g	wild garlic leaves
2oz/50g	pack of fresh dill, finely chopped
	TO SERVE
	fresh bread

Bring a small saucepan of water to boil and drop in the fava beans. Cook for 4–5 minutes, until soft. Drain the beans and allow to cool. Reserve half a cup of the water that the beans were cooked in.

When the beans are cool enough to handle, remove and discard the outer skins.

Heat the olive oil in a deep frying pan, and over low heat cook the fennel and shallots with the sugar sprinkled on top for 10 minutes, stirring from time to time. Next, add the wild garlic leaves and cook for a further 5 minutes. Season to taste and remove from the heat. If wild garlic is out of season, use wild arugula, which will give a light, peppery taste.

Place the cooked fava beans in a food processor with the cooked fennel, shallots, and wild garlic and blend to a smooth purée. Add the reserved water as required, until you achieve the consistency of heavy cream.

Sprinkle with the fresh dill and serve with fresh bread.

For 8–10 to share

Sumac Scallops with Walnut and Roasted Garlic Sauce

This is particularly delicious served with chili cress, but if you can't get any, ordinary cress will do.

FOR THE SAUCE

1 garlic bulb

7oz/200g walnuts, finely ground

3 tablespoons olive oil

zest and juice of 1 small lemon

¾ cup/200ml chicken stock

FOR THE SCALLOPS

16 medium-sized scallops

2 tablespoons olive oil

1 teaspoon ground sumac

TO SERVE

2 pots of chili cress

2oz/50g walnut pieces, toasted

TO MAKE THE SAUCE

Preheat the oven to 400°F (350°F fan)/200°C (180°C fan).

Place the whole garlic bulb on a small baking tray and roast in the oven for 20 minutes. Remove, and when cool enough to handle, squeeze the roasted garlic flesh out of the bulb, discarding the skin.

In a small saucepan, mix together the garlic, walnuts, olive oil, lemon zest, and juice, until you have a smooth creamy mixture. On medium heat, stirring all the time, add the chicken stock. Cook for 5 minutes and season to taste.

TO COOK THE SCALLOPS

Brush the scallops with olive oil. Heat a nonstick frying pan over medium heat and cook the scallops for 2 minutes on each side. Remove from the heat and sprinkle with sumac.

TO SERVE

Arrange the hot scallops on a platter. Drizzle with the walnut and garlic sauce and scatter with some chili cress and toasted walnuts.

For 8 to share

Sumac Crab and Avocado
with Tahini Dressing

FOR THE DRESSING

1 egg

²/₃ cup/150ml olive oil

juice of 1 lemon

3½oz/100g fresh brown crabmeat, cooked

1 tablespoon tahini

FOR THE CRAB

1lb/450g fresh white crabmeat, cooked

juice of ½ lemon

1 teaspoon ground sumac

2oz/50g pack of fresh basil, leaves only, finely chopped

2oz/50g pack of fresh parsley, leaves only, finely chopped

2 large avocados

extra lemon juice for the avocados

TO SERVE

black sesame crisp flatbread (see p.169)

2 lemons, cut into quarters

TO MAKE THE DRESSING

Whisk the egg, drizzling in the olive oil at the same time, until you have a thick consistency. Add the lemon juice and the cooked brown crabmeat. Combine and season well before finally stirring in the tahini.

TO PREPARE THE CRAB

Combine the cooked white crabmeat, lemon juice, sumac, and herbs, and season to taste. Peel and thinly slice the avocados, squeezing lemon juice over the top to prevent discoloration if not using immediately.

TO SERVE

Top pieces of Black Sesame Crisp Flatbread with some of the sumac crab and the avocado slices, and drizzle with the tahini dressing. Serve with lemon quarters.

For 8 to share

Lemon Balm Sorbet, Black Sesame Macaroon Crumble, and Lemon Balm Oil

FOR THE SORBET

2½ cups/600ml water

⅔ cup/160ml light corn syrup

small bunch of lemon balm, leaves only

½ cup/110g superfine sugar

juice of 2 lemons

FOR THE CRUMBLE

2oz/50g ground black sesame seeds

3oz/80g ground almonds

2 cups/220g confectioner's sugar

3 medium egg whites

2 tablespoons superfine sugar

FOR THE OIL

1 bunch lemon balm

scant ½ cup/100ml canola oil

TO SERVE

12–16 small lemon balm leaves

1 DAY IN ADVANCE

Blend the water and syrup together in a food processor or a blender. Pour into a saucepan and heat gently. Remove from the heat just before it boils. Add the lemon balm leaves, sugar, and lemon juice. Stir until the sugar dissolves and allow to cool. You can leave the balm leaves in or discard as you choose.

Using an ice cream maker, churn the mixture as per your machine's instructions, for about 40–45 minutes. If you haven't got an ice cream maker, place the mixture in a plastic container, cover, and place in the freezer. You'll need to stir the sorbet every half an hour until it's set.

TO MAKE THE CRUMBLE

Preheat the oven to 350°F (300°F fan)/170°C (150°C fan).

Blend the sesame seeds, ground almonds, and confectioner's sugar in a food processor. Whisk the egg whites to hard peaks, add the superfine sugar, and continue whisking until glossy. Fold the sesame mixture into the egg whites a little at a time.

Line and lightly grease an 8 × 11in/20 × 27cm baking tray. Spread the macaroon mixture over the tray—it should be about 1in/2cm thick. Bake in the oven for 45 minutes. Remove and cool. Break into crumbled pieces and put to one side until needed.

TO MAKE THE OIL

Place the lemon balm into a food processor and blend until finely chopped. Add the canola oil and pulse briefly to combine. Pour the mixture through a sieve and discard the solids, reserving only the scented oil.

TO SERVE

Arrange a few pieces of the macaroon crumble on each plate. Spoon on some lemon balm sorbet, drizzle with a touch of lemon balm oil, then scatter more of the crumble on top. Garnish with lemon balm leaves and serve.

For 8 to share

Sweet Eucalyptus & Liquid Gold

CARDAMOM AND HONEY

The great thing about **cardamom** is that it can be used in savory and sweet dishes. For me it is both sweet and reminiscent of eucalyptus. Available in green and black varieties; ground, in whole pods, or just the seeds. A member of the ginger family, it is highly perfumed, so you need to be careful how much you use. As part of a marinade, added to goat's cheese with a hint of maple syrup, sprinkled on baked figs, combined in a white chocolate mousse, or simply added to your freshly ground coffee, it makes a dish exquisite.

There are almost as many types of **honey** as there are flowers. Mono floral honeys are more distinctive, for example heather, acacia, lavender, and orange blossom. Try a few until you find one that you really like, or of course you can stick to the more commonly sold poly floral honey which is derived from a variety of flowers.

It might sound self-evident, but honey has a delicate natural sweetness, completely different from manufactured sugars, that lends itself to all things culinary. It's incredibly versatile: drizzled on simple böreks, stirred into yogurt, or, for a sensational display of flavors, try the Lemon Thyme Infused Burrata with Honey, Berries, and Balsamic Vinegar (see p. 142).

Honey Mashed Fava Beans
with Capers and Scallions

This recipe needs at least 6 hours in the fridge to set, so make sure you prepare
it well in advance. This is one of the most common Turkish mezze in any main
street eaterie.

9oz/250g dried fava beans, soaked
overnight

3 shallots, finely chopped

2 garlic cloves, crushed

7 tablespoons olive oil

1 bay leaf

½ teaspoon turmeric

4 scallions, finely sliced

2 tablespoons small capers,
drained

zest and juice of ½ lemon

1 teaspoon runny honey

8–10 sprigs of fresh dill, finely
chopped

TO SERVE

1 tablespoon capers, chopped,
or use baby capers if you can

6–8 parsley sprigs, chopped

2 tablespoons olive oil

½ teaspoon nigella seeds

To ensure a smooth and silky purée, remove the skins from the pre-soaked
fava beans. If they're not loose enough, boil for 10 minutes, drain, and cool
before removing them.

In a large pan, sauté the shallots and garlic for 2 minutes in 4 tablespoons of
the olive oil over medium heat. Add the bay leaf, turmeric, and shelled fava
beans. Season to taste, then cover with 4 cups/1 liter of water. Simmer for
about 1 hour, or until the beans are soft and the cooking liquid has mostly
evaporated. Remove and discard the bay leaf.

In a small frying pan, sauté the scallions and capers for 2–3 minutes in
2 tablespoons of olive oil on medium heat. Transfer to a food processor along
with the cooked beans and blend until smooth. Check the seasoning, then
add the lemon zest, lemon juice, and honey.

Using the remaining olive oil, brush a shallow rectangular tray approx.
8 × 12in/20 × 30cm then line the sides and base with plastic wrap, brush
them with oil, and scatter with the chopped dill. Pour in the bean purée,
smooth over the top, cover with plastic wrap, and place in the fridge for at
least 6 hours to set.

TO SERVE

Meanwhile, combine in a bowl the nigella seeds, capers, parsley, and oil, and
mix. When ready to serve, cut out small round shapes with a pastry cutter.
Turn the rounds over so that the dill is on top. Serve cold, sprinkled with the
capers and seeds mixture.

For 6 to share

Raki and Honey Cured Salmon

This recipe is very simple, but you'll need to plan it 2 days in advance.
If you can't find raki, vodka can be used as a substitute.

2 tablespoons/25g light
    brown sugar

2oz/50g sea salt

¼ tablespoon dill seeds

½ small bunch of fresh dill,
    finely chopped

½ small bunch of fresh
    oregano, finely chopped

5–6 fresh oregano flowers,
    finely chopped

1–1⅓lb/500–600g fillet of
    salmon

1 teaspoon runny honey

3 tablespoons raki

TO SERVE

micro red amaranth
leaves or any micro-
greens

fresh herb salad

2 DAYS IN ADVANCE

In a bowl, combine the sugar, salt, dill seeds, fresh dill, fresh oregano, and oregano flowers. Having made sure that there are no bones remaining in the fish, lay the fillet skin side down on a large piece of plastic wrap. Press the dill and oregano mixture into the fish, drizzle with the honey, and spoon over the raki. Enclose the fish in the plastic wrap in such a way as not to let the curing mixture escape. Place the fillet on a board, then cover with a second, weighted down with some cans. Refrigerate for 36 hours, turning every 12 hours.

After 36 hours remove the fish from the plastic wrap, scrape off and discard the curing ingredients if you wish—I like to leave it for a crunchy effect—and pat dry with paper towels. Re-wrap the fish in plastic wrap and put back into the fridge, unweighted, for a further 12 hours.

After a total of 48 hours' curing, finely slice the salmon and serve with amaranth cress leaves and a fresh herb salad.

For 8 to share

Pistachio and Cardamom Lamb Manti

Manti are filled pasta dumplings and are extremely popular in Turkey. The dough is usually made using just plain flour, but this version, shown to me at the Çiragan Palace, also uses pistachios, giving the dumplings a wonderful taste and intriguing bright green color. Served hot, topped with yogurt and a drizzle of paprika oil, these are fabulous. This recipe does take some time to make, but it is well worth it. I like to make double quantities and freeze some. You will need a pasta machine, although a rolling pin can also be used.

FOR THE DOUGH

2½ cups/400g bread flour, plus extra for dusting

1 teaspoon sea salt

¼ teaspoon cardamom seeds, finely ground

2oz/60g pistachios, finely ground

4 eggs, lightly beaten

¼ cup/50ml water

FOR THE FILLING

7oz/200g ground lamb

2 shallots, finely diced

1 garlic clove, crushed

¼ teaspoon ground cinnamon

small bunch of fresh mint, leaves only, finely chopped

3 tablespoons hummus (see p.174)

1 HOUR IN ADVANCE

Using the dough hook in your food processor, combine the flour, salt, cardamom, and pistachios, adding the eggs and water a little at a time to form a dough. Remove and knead the dough for 8–10 minutes, until silky smooth. Wrap in plastic wrap and allow to rest for 1 hour.

TO MAKE THE FILLING

Combine all the ingredients, except for the hummus, in a bowl. Put to one side until ready to use.

TO MAKE THE MANTI

Cut the dough into 4 pieces. Lightly dust with flour, then pass each piece of dough through a pasta machine several times on the thickest setting, until it's beautifully smooth. Reduce the setting and pass through again, repeating until the dough is very fine. This process can be done with a rolling pin, but it is much more difficult and doesn't produce as fine results.

Cut the dough pieces into about 80 squares, roughly 1in/3cm wide (or 1in/3cm diameter rounds). Place a small amount of filling in to the center of each square and top with a little hummus. Wet the edges of the squares with water, then pull the corners up and pinch the edges together to form a sealed pyramid-shaped parcel.

Place the manti on a lightly floured baking tray and refrigerate until ready to cook.

1 cup/200g thick yogurt or suzme
             (strained yogurt, see p. 182)

1 garlic clove, crushed

4 tablespoons olive oil

1 teaspoon sweet paprika

Bring a pan of salted water to a boil and drop in the manti, a few at a time, taking care not to overload the pan. Cook for 3 minutes, remove, drain, and keep warm.

TO SERVE

Combine the yogurt and garlic, and season to taste. Serve the manti hot, topped with a generous spoonful of yogurt. Mix the olive oil and paprika together and drizzle all over the yogurt.

For 8 to share

Kadaifi Wrapped Goat's Cheese and Cardamom Figs with Thyme Flowers

7oz/200g soft, mild goat's cheese

2 tablespoons mascarpone

2 tablespoons maple syrup

¼ teaspoon ground cardamom

11oz/300g kadaifi pastry

5 tablespoons melted butter

18 fresh ripe figs

2oz/50g pack of fresh thyme, with
          flowers

1 egg yolk, beaten for brushing

Preheat the oven to 425°F (400°F fan)/220°C (200°C fan).

Combine the goat's cheese, mascarpone, maple syrup, and cardamom in a bowl.

Carefully unfold the kadaifi and spread it out lengthways. Divide into 18 long strands—you will have some waste—and give each a generous brushing with the melted butter. Using a sharp knife, make a small cross over the top of each fig and squeeze open slightly, like a flower. Top with some of the cheese and maple syrup mixture.

Arrange the figs on a large, foil-lined baking tray and, starting at the bottom, wrap a thick single strand of butter-brushed kadaifi around each fig, leaving just the cheese-filled top exposed. Brush the strands of kadaifi with the egg yolk.

Bake the figs in the oven for 7–8 minutes, until the kadaifi is golden and the cheese melted. Remove from the oven and sprinkle with the thyme flowers before serving.

For 8 to share

Mung Bean Salad with Spicy Roasted Tomato and Honey Dressing

This dish is served daily at the Çiya restaurants of Kadýköy, Istanbul.
Sometimes they add chargrilled red peppers or eggplants, turning this salad
into a substantial meal.

FOR THE DRESSING

5 ripe tomatoes, halved

2/3 cup/150ml olive oil

1 small garlic clove, crushed

1in/2cm fresh ginger, peeled and grated

juice of 1 lemon

1 tablespoon runny honey

FOR THE SALAD

14oz/400g mung beans, soaked overnight

8 scallions, sliced

3 plum tomatoes, cubed

small bunch of fresh parsley, finely chopped

½ teaspoon red chili flakes

TO MAKE THE DRESSING

Preheat the oven to 400°F (350°F fan)/200°C (180°C fan).

Arrange the tomatoes on a roasting tray, season, and drizzle with 1
tablespoon of the olive oil. Roast in the oven for 30 minutes, then remove
and allow to cool.

Place the cooled tomatoes in a food processor with the garlic, ginger, lemon
juice, and honey. Blend while slowly drizzling in the remaining olive oil until
you have a smooth consistency.

TO PREPARE THE SALAD

Drain the beans and place in a pan. Cover them with cold water, bring to
a boil, then reduce to a simmer and cook for 20–30 minutes, until soft. Drain
and cool.

Place the cooled beans, scallions, plum tomatoes, and parsley in a large bowl
and toss gently. Sprinkle with the chili flakes, then drizzle with some of the
dressing. You will have about 2 cups/475ml of dressing, so if you have some
left over, store it in a jar and refrigerate.

For 6 to share

Grilled Shrimp, Fig, and Goat's Cheese Salad with Lemon and Honey Dressing

FOR THE SALAD

16 raw jumbo shrimp, shells and
    heads removed, deveined

1 teaspoon ground sumac

1 teaspoon za'atar

5 tablespoons melted butter

4 fresh ripe figs, sliced into
   8 wedges each

7oz/200g goat's cheese, crumbled

FOR THE DRESSING

3 tablespoons balsamic
   vinegar

2 teaspoons runny honey

2 tablespoons olive oil

   juice of 1 lemon

TO SERVE

1 tablespoon black sesame
   seeds

   a few apple blossom flowers
   or any herb flowers or leaves

TO MAKE THE SALAD

Preheat the broiler.

Place the shrimp in a bowl with the sumac, za'atar, and most of the butter. Mix well. Place the shrimp on an ovenproof tray under the broiler and cook for about 5 minutes, turning halfway through to cook evenly. Remove to a serving platter and brush with the remaining butter. Scatter with the figs and goat's cheese and season to taste.

TO MAKE THE DRESSING

Mix together all the ingredients and drizzle over the shrimp. Finish off by sprinkling with the black sesame seeds. Garnish with a few apple blossom flowers. If you cannot get any, you can use any herb flowers.

For 8 to share

Honey and Ginger Roasted Apricots with Ricotta on Green Peppercorn and Za'atar Spiced Filo

6 ripe apricots, quartered

1in/3cm fresh ginger, peeled and grated

3 tablespoons runny honey

4 large rectangular sheets of filo pastry

4 tablespoons/50g melted butter

1 teaspoon green peppercorns, crushed

2–3 tablespoons za'atar

14oz/400g fresh ricotta, crumbled

Preheat the oven to 400°F (350°F fan)/200°C (180°C fan).

In a bowl, toss together the apricots, ginger, and honey. Arrange on a baking tray and cook in the oven for 8 minutes, until just soft and lightly golden. Keep warm with the cooking juices until ready to serve.

Arrange a sheet of filo on your work surface, brush with butter, and sprinkle with green peppercorns and za'atar. Top with another sheet of filo and repeat. Do this until all 4 sheets are layered on top of each other with the peppercorns and za'atar sprinkled in between. Cut the layers horizontally into 5 equal strips, then vertically, so that you end up with 25 squares, although you actually only need 24.

Arrange the squares onto a greased baking sheet, then weight it down with another baking tray on top and place in the oven for 8–10 minutes, until crispy and golden.

TO SERVE

Crumble the ricotta onto 12 small serving plates, then arrange 2 ginger roasted apricots on each plate and garnish with a couple of the spiced filo pieces. Finally, drizzle with the apricot cooking juices.

Serves 12 as small bites

Nine Spice Lamb with Honey, Red Onion, and Fig Compote

FOR THE MARINADE

juice of 1 lime

3 tablespoons olive oil

1 teaspoon baharat (see p. 173)

8 lamb chops, about 1in/2cm thick, fat trimmed off

FOR THE COMPOTE

1½ tablespoons/20g butter

4 red onions, thinly sliced

½ teaspoon sugar

1 teaspoon honey

6 large fresh ripe figs, cut into thin wedges

3½ tablespoons/50ml sherry vinegar

1 tablespoon olive oil

2 tablespoons soy sauce

1 teaspoon za'atar

2 HOURS IN ADVANCE

Combine the lime juice, olive oil, and baharat in a bowl. Rub into the lamb, place in a covered dish, and leave in the fridge to marinate for 2 hours.

TO MAKE THE COMPOTE

In a pan, melt the butter on low heat. Add the onions, sprinkle with the sugar, and drizzle in the honey. Stir well, cover, and cook for 15 minutes on very low heat, making sure the onions do not color. Remove the lid and add the figs and half of the sherry vinegar. Continue cooking, uncovered, until the liquid has almost evaporated. Add the remaining sherry vinegar and continue cooking until the liquid has evaporated. Finally, stir in the olive oil and soy sauce—you should be left with a sticky jam consistency. Remove from the heat, mix in the za'atar, and allow to cool.

In a hot griddle pan, cook the marinated lamb chops on high heat, for 2–4 minutes on each side, until golden brown. The cooking time depends on how you like your lamb, so cook for longer if you prefer them well done.

Arrange a spiced lamb chop on top of a generous helping of the red onion and fig compote.

For 8 to share

Lemon Thyme Infused Burrata with Honey, Berries, and Balsamic Vinegar

1lb/450g burrata (or mozzarella if burrata is not available)

6 lemon thyme sprigs, leaves only

4 tablespoons runny honey

3 tablespoons almonds, toasted

14oz/400g mixed fresh berries

6 fresh ripe figs, cut into thin wedges

3 tablespoons balsamic vinegar

1 tablespoon confectioner's sugar

1 DAY IN ADVANCE

Place burrata in a bowl with the lemon thyme leaves and 1 tablespoon of honey. Cover and leave in the fridge overnight.

TO SERVE

Spoon the lemon thyme infused cheese onto a serving platter. Drizzle with the remaining honey, then sprinkle on the almonds, berries, and figs. Finish by drizzling with just a little balsamic vinegar and dusting with confectioner's sugar.

For 8 to share

Orange and Honey Glazed Eggplant Rolls with Apricot and Cottage Cheese

FOR THE FILLING

zest of 1 orange

3½oz/100g *dried apricots, finely chopped*

3½oz/100g *cottage cheese*

2 *tablespoons thick yogurt or suzme (strained yogurt, see p.182)*

1 *teaspoon ground cumin*

1 *teaspoon ground sumac*

¼ *teaspoon cinnamon*

2oz/50g *pack of fresh parsley, finely chopped*

FOR THE ROLLS

juice of ½ orange

1 *teaspoon runny honey*

2 *tablespoons olive oil*

2 *medium eggplants, sliced lengthways into ¼in/½cm thick pieces*

TO MAKE THE FILLING

In a bowl, combine the orange zest, apricots, cottage cheese, yogurt or suzme, cumin, sumac, and cinnamon, and season to taste. Add the parsley and mix again.

TO PREPARE THE ROLLS

Combine the orange juice and honey in a bowl, and put to one side ready to use. Lightly oil a griddle pan and place on medium/high heat. Arrange the eggplant slices on the griddle and brush with the orange and honey mixture. Cook for 2–3 minutes, then turn them over, brush again, and cook for a further 2–3 minutes, until they are a golden brown. You may need to do this in batches if your griddle pan isn't big enough.

Spoon some filling onto each of the eggplant slices and roll each slice up to enclose the filling. Arrange the rolls on a serving platter and brush with the remaining orange juice and honey before serving.

Makes 16–18, depending on size of eggplants

Cardamom and White Chocolate Mousse

Make these a day in advance so they can chill overnight. Be sure to use the freshest, free-range eggs.

4 eggs, separated

100g superfine sugar

14oz/400g white chocolate, broken into pieces

1¼ cups/300ml heavy cream

½ teaspoon ground cardamom

1 teaspoon cocoa powder, for dusting

1 DAY IN ADVANCE

In a food processor, blend the egg yolks with all but a tablespoon of the sugar until thick and creamy.

Half fill a saucepan with water, bring to a boil, then turn down to a simmer. Put the chocolate into a heatproof bowl and place it on top of the simmering water (it shouldn't actually touch the water). Give the chocolate a stir from time to time, until it has melted. Allow the melted chocolate to cool, then combine with the egg and sugar mixture.

Whisk the egg whites, adding the remaining tablespoon of sugar, and beat until shiny.

Whip the heavy cream and fold into the egg and chocolate mixture. Finally, gently fold in the whisked egg whites and the cardamom. Do not stir, beat, or whisk any further, as the object is to get as much air as possible into the mixture.

Pour the mixture into 8 small ramekins and refrigerate overnight.

Dust with the cocoa powder before serving.

Makes 8

Sticky Honey, Pomegranate, and Ottoman-Spiced Chicken Wings

4 tablespoons pomegranate molasses (see p. 175)

juice of 1 fresh pomegranate

1 tablespoon runny honey

2 garlic cloves, crushed

2lb/1kg chicken wings

FOR THE OTTOMAN SPICE

1 tablespoon ground oregano

1 tablespoon ground mint

½ teaspoon ground black pepper

¼ tablespoon ground cinnamon

1 tablespoon ground cumin

¼ tablespoon ground ginger

¼ tablespoon ground fennel

¼ tablespoon ground allspice

½ tablespoon ground sumac

TO SERVE

seeds of 1 pomegranate

4 HOURS IN ADVANCE

Combine the pomegranate molasses, pomegranate juice, honey, and garlic in a bowl. Add the chicken wings and thoroughly coat with the pomegranate marinade. Cover and refrigerate for at least 4 hours or overnight.

Meanwhile, mix all the spices together.

Preheat the oven to 400°F (350°F fan)/200°C (180°C fan).

Arrange the marinated chicken wings on a large baking tray and sprinkle liberally with the Ottoman spice blend, putting aside a little for later. Roast for 30–40 minutes, until golden. Sprinkle on the remaining spice and pomegranate seeds just before serving.

Serve with Caramelized Onion Salad with Sumac and Pomegranate Dressing (see p. 88).

For 8 to share

Pistachio Yogurt Cake with White Chocolate and Cardamom Frosting

FOR THE CAKE

7oz/200g pistachios, ground

½ teaspoon ground cardamom

11 tablespoons/150g unsalted butter, cubed

1½ cups/225g self-rising flour

1 cup/183g superfine sugar

3 eggs

½ cup/125ml thick yogurt or suzme (strained yogurt, see p. 182)

FOR THE FROSTING

3½oz/100g white chocolate, chopped

7oz/200g cream cheese

½ teaspoon rose water

1 tablespoon confectioner's sugar

¼ teaspoon ground cardamom

1–2 small edible roses, petals only

1 tablespoon confectioner's sugar (for sprinkling)

Preheat the oven to 400°F (350°F fan)/200°C (180°C fan). Butter and line an 8in/20cm cake pan with parchment paper.

Using a food processor, blend the ground pistachios, cardamom, butter, flour, and sugar until you have something resembling breadcrumbs. Tip into a mixing bowl and combine with the eggs and yogurt or suzme. Pour the mixture into the prepared cake pan and bake in the oven for 1 hour. Cover the cake with foil halfway through cooking. Allow to cool on a rack.

TO MAKE THE FROSTING

Melt the chocolate in a bowl over a saucepan of simmering water and allow to cool. In a separate bowl, combine the cream cheese with the rose water, then add the cooled chocolate. Sift in the confectioner's sugar and sprinkle in the ground cardamom. Mix well until you have a smooth cream.

Serve cake accompanied by the chocolate and cardamom cream. Sprinkle with edible roses and dust with confectioner's sugar. Serve.

For 8–10 to share

Exotic Perfume *&* Delicate Fragrances

CINNAMON AND FLOWERS

Many years ago I was walking around a spice market in Mauritius, and there, among the heavenly scents, I bought a small bag of cinnamon bark. I put it into an ornate wooden box and brought it home with me. It has never been used, but still sits in its box on my desk; every now and then, I open it up and its exotic perfume instantly transports me back to that spice market.

Ground **cinnamon**, the most common form in which this spice is found, is a major constituent in many spice blends, baharat in particular. It's used across the Eastern Mediterranean in both sweet and savory dishes, marinades, pilafs, baklavas, and cakes.

What could possibly be more inspiring and exciting than using **flowers** in cooking? The vibrancy of their color, the distinctive perfumed flavor, the delicate pretty fragrance: everything to delight the senses, alluring and seductive. Fresh or dried, flowers can lift the ordinary into the extraordinary.

Not all flowers are edible of course, but of those that are, nasturtiums, roses, and lavender are the most common in Eastern Mediterranean cuisine.* Not to forget those that you will find in the herb garden: the purple flowers of chives, the snowy white cilantro flowers, the violet basil flowers, and the flaming orange zucchini flowers, to name but a few.

As a child, I knew nothing of strawberry jam; instead I grew up on rose petal jam for breakfast and rose petal or hibiscus ice cream as an after-dinner treat. Arguably, the best roses in the world come from the Eastern Mediterranean, and they are absolutely delicious as part of a spice blend to go with cauliflower or made into a syrup to accompany figs and ricotta.

*Only use commercially grown culinary flowers, or those from your own garden—others may have been sprayed with pesticides.

Orange blossom water is exactly what you would expect it to be. Distilled from an infusion of the fragrant blossoms of the orange tree, it is floral, bittersweet and, unsurprisingly, citrusy orange in flavor. It can be added to yogurts and aioli, drizzled on to fruit salads, and used in marinades. Readily available, it is usually very concentrated, so you'll need to go steady with it.

Lavender flowers can be used fresh or dried, and are fragrant, sweet, citrusy, even slightly woody in flavor. Add a touch to white chocolate, or even to chicken or lamb dishes. Seal the flowers in a jar of sugar for a couple of weeks and use the resultant lavender sugar in cakes. The dried flowers are much more potent than the fresh, so use a little at a time—you can always add more later.

Cauliflower with Rose Petal Spice Blend and Cardamom Hollandaise

FOR THE SPICE BLEND

- 1 tablespoon dried rose petals
- ½ teaspoon ground allspice
- ½ teaspoon ground cinnamon
- ½ teaspoon za'atar
- ¼ teaspoon ground cardamom

FOR THE CAULIFLOWER

- 2 tablespoons extra virgin olive oil
- 1 large cauliflower, cut into florets

FOR THE HOLLANDAISE

- 3 egg yolks
- 1 tablespoon lemon juice
- 12 tablespoons/175g melted butter
- ¼ teaspoon ground cardamom
  dried rose petals

TO MAKE THE SPICE BLEND

Combine the dried rose petals and ground spices together.

TO COOK THE CAULIFLOWER

In a large pan, heat the olive oil on high and sauté the cauliflower florets for 6–8 minutes over medium heat, until golden brown. Place in a serving dish and sprinkle with the spice blend.

FOR THE HOLLANDAISE

Half fill a blender with boiling water, allow to stand for 3 minutes, then throw the water away and shake dry. Place the egg yolks and lemon juice in the warmed blender and blend for 10 seconds. With the machine still running, slowly drizzle in the melted butter through the hole in the lid. Blend until the sauce becomes thick and smooth. Finally, stir in the cardamom. Pour the hollandaise over the cauliflower, sprinkle with rose petals, and serve.

For 6–8 to share

Lemon Vanilla Custard Baklava
with Orange Blossom Syrup

FOR THE SYRUP

- ¾ cup/250g superfine sugar
- 1 cup/250ml water
- zest and juice of 1 small lemon
- 1 tablespoon orange blossom flower water

FOR THE BAKLAVA

- 4 eggs
- 1 cup/200g superfine sugar
- 3 cups/750ml milk
- ¾ cup/200ml fine semolina
- zest and juice of 3 lemons
- 2 vanilla pods, seeds scraped
- 14 tablespoons/100g melted butter, and extra for brushing
- 9oz/250g filo pastry

TO MAKE THE SYRUP

In a saucepan, dissolve the sugar in the water over medium heat until it becomes syrupy. Add the lemon juice, zest, and orange blossom water, stir, and allow to cool completely.

TO PREPARE THE BAKLAVA

Preheat the oven to 400°F (350°F fan)/200°C (180°C fan).

Half-fill a pan (large enough to sit a mixing bowl on top of) with water and bring to a boil. Reduce to a simmer. Meanwhile, in a bowl, beat together the eggs and sugar. In a separate pan, boil the milk. Remove from the heat and

whisk in the egg and sugar mixture. Stir in the semolina and transfer to a mixing bowl. Place the bowl on top of the pan of simmering water and stir for 10–15 minutes, gradually adding the melted butter, until the mixture thickens to a custard. Remove from the heat and stir in the lemon juice and zest and the vanilla.

Butter an ovenproof dish, about 8 × 12in/20 × 30cm. Lay in the first of the filo sheets, cutting or adding pastry to cover the base of the dish, then brush with butter. Repeat, brushing with butter as you go, until you have used half the sheets. Now pour in the custard, and layer in the rest of the sheets, again buttering between each sheet.

Using a sharp knife, cut any pattern you desire (diamonds, squares etc.) all the way through the pastry, then place in the oven for 15 minutes. Reduce the heat to 350°F (325°F fan)/180°C (160°C fan) and bake for a further 30 minutes, until golden. Remove the lemon custard baklava from the oven and pour the cooled lemon syrup over the top.

Allow to set for at least 4 hours and serve cold.

For 8–10 to share

Cinnamon and Black Sesame Crusted Cod
with Baby Fennel and Radish Salad

FOR THE COD

1¾lb/800g cod fillet, cut into long thin strips, approx. 1in/3cm thick

2 tablespoons olive oil

1 teaspoon ground cinnamon

4 tablespoons black sesame seeds

3 tablespoons olive oil extra, for cooking

FOR THE SALAD

8 baby fennel bulbs

16 pink radishes, thinly sliced

1 red onion, finely sliced

tomato and sumac dressing (see p.179)

TO PREPARE THE COD

Season the cod strips with salt and pepper and brush with the olive oil. Mix the cinnamon and black sesame seeds together and use to coat the fish. Put to one side until ready to cook.

TO MAKE THE SALAD

Slice the baby fennel bulbs wafer thin. Combine the fennel in a bowl with the radishes and onion.

TO COOK THE COD

In a frying pan, heat the olive oil and fry the cod strips for 2–3 minutes on medium heat, turning until golden on all sides.

Serve the cod hot, on a bed of the salad and drizzled with Tomato and Sumac Dressing.

For 8 to share

Lavender Chocolate and Pistachio Mousse

9oz/250g good quality chocolate
(70% cocoa solids), chopped

5 egg yolks

3½oz/100g pistachios, finely ground

1²/₃ cups/400ml whipping cream

¼ teaspoon lavender essence

2oz/50g pistachios, roughly chopped,
toasted

TO SERVE

2oz/50g pistachios, crushed

4 HOURS IN ADVANCE

Using a double boiler or a heatproof bowl sitting over the top of a saucepan of boiling water, slowly melt the chocolate. Once melted, cool slightly and whisk in the egg yolks. Fold in the ground pistachios. At this stage your chocolate will look like it has curdled. Please don't worry, once you have added the cream, the chocolate will become smooth and silky again.

In a separate bowl, whip the cream to soft peaks. Add the lavender essence, then gently fold the lavender cream into the chocolate mixture.

Spoon into small glasses and top with toasted pistachios. Refrigerate for 30 minutes. If you chill overnight, please allow to rest at room temperature for at least an hour before serving.

TO SERVE

Serve cold, sprinkled with pistachios.

For 8 to share

Roasted Figs with Orange Blossom, Passion Fruit, and Mint Sauce

juice of 3 oranges

1 teaspoon orange blossom water

12 fresh ripe figs

3 tablespoons raw or natural sugar, such as demerara

TO SERVE

¾ cup/200ml thick yogurt or suzme (strained yogurt, see p.182)

6 passion fruits, pulp only

3–4 sprigs of fresh mint, leaves only, finely chopped

1 tablespoon confectioner's sugar

Preheat the oven to 400°F (350°F fan)/200°C (180°C fan).

In a bowl, combine the orange juice with the orange blossom water. Cut a cross in the top of each fig and squeeze open the figs very slightly. You'll need a baking tray in which the whole figs will sit without much room to move around. Arrange them on the tray, then pour the orange juice mixture over the top of the figs and sprinkle with the sugar. Bake in the oven for 15 minutes. Remove from the oven and cool.

TO SERVE

Put the yogurt or suzme into a bowl and combine with the passion fruit pulp and fresh mint. Plate up the figs and spoon some of the passion fruit yogurt on top. Dust with confectioner's sugar.

For 6 to share

Roast Potatoes with Rosemary, Shallot, and Orange Blossom Aioli

2lb/1kg potatoes, peeled and cut into chunks

3 shallots

5 tablespoons olive oil

½ tablespoon sea salt

FOR THE AIOLI

4 sprigs of fresh rosemary, leaves only

²/₃ cup/150ml olive oil

2 egg yolks

juice of ½ orange

zest of 1 orange

½ teaspoon orange blossom water

Preheat the oven to 400°F (350°F fan)/200°C (180°C fan).

Cook the potatoes in a pan of boiling water until they are a little more than half cooked. Drain and tip into a roasting pan. Throw in the shallots, still in their skins, drizzle with the olive oil, and season with the sea salt. Place in the oven for about 1½ hours, until the potatoes are golden and crispy. Remove the shallots after about 45 minutes. Once they have cooled enough to handle, squeeze the flesh out of the skins and put to one side.

TO MAKE THE AIOLI

Roughly bruise the rosemary leaves to bring out their flavor. Pour half the olive oil into a small pan and heat until just before it starts to really bubble. Remove from the heat and throw in the rosemary leaves. Allow to infuse for 1 hour, then add the remaining olive oil. Sieve to remove the leaves. Discard them and reserve the oil.

Place the egg yolks in a food processor with the shallot flesh. Purée until smooth and then, with the machine still running, slowly drizzle in the infused rosemary oil. Season, then add the orange juice, zest, and orange blossom water.

Serve the roasted potatoes with the rosemary and roasted shallot aioli.

For 8 to share

Rose Water Infused Saffron and Cardamom Spiced Lamb Wraps with Tahini Sumac Mayonnaise

FOR THE LAMB

½ teaspoon black pepper, crushed

½ teaspoon cayenne pepper

¼ teaspoon ground coriander

½ teaspoon ground cumin

¼ teaspoon ground ginger

¼ teaspoon ground cinnamon

⅛ teaspoon ground nutmeg

3⅓lb/1½kg lamb shoulder

6 threads of saffron

3 tablespoons rose water

3 tablespoons olive oil

8 cardamom pods, crushed

1 cup/250ml water

FOR TAHINI SUMAC MAYONNAISE

3 egg yolks

⅔ cup/150ml peanut oil

⅔ cup/150ml olive oil

1 tablespoon tahini

juice ½ lemon

½ teaspoon sumac

TO SERVE

24 small round flatbreads

1 DAY IN ADVANCE

Combine the black pepper, cayenne pepper, coriander, cumin, ginger, cinnamon, and nutmeg in a bowl. Rub the spices into the shoulder of lamb, then cover and place in the fridge overnight.

3 HOURS IN ADVANCE

Preheat the oven to 300°F (250°F fan)/150°C (130°C fan).

Soak the saffron threads in the rose water for 10 minutes. In a large ovenproof pan, heat the olive oil and brown the marinated lamb for 5–10 minutes, turning so that it is brown on all sides. Remove from the heat and add the saffron rose water, cardamom, and water. Tightly cover the pan with foil, then place in the oven and cook for 3 hours. Take care when you remove the foil, as a lot of steam will have built up. The lamb, once cooked, should be falling off the bone.

TO MAKE THE MAYONNAISE

Whisk the egg yolks in a bowl, then, still whisking, drizzle in the oils a little at a time until you have a thick mayonnaise. Add the tahini and lemon juice and season to taste. Spoon into a bowl and sprinkle with sumac.

TO SERVE

Once the lamb has cooled, shred the meat. Warm the flatbreads then place a generous amount of meat in the center of each one, spoon on some tahini mayonnaise, and serve.

For 8 to share

Seven Spice Ground Beef and Zucchinis with Garlic Yogurt Sauce

FOR THE SEVEN SPICE

- ½ teaspoon ground cinnamon
- ¼ teaspoon ground allspice
- ¼ teaspoon crushed black pepper
- ¼ teaspoon ground cloves
- ¼ teaspoon ground coriander
- ¼ teaspoon ground nutmeg

    pinch of white pepper

FOR THE BEEF

- 2 tablespoons olive oil
- 1 onion, finely chopped
- 1⅓lb/600g ground beef
- 3 medium zucchinis, cut lengthways into thin slices

    small bunch of fresh mint, leaves only, chopped

FOR THE SAUCE

- 2 cups/400g thick yogurt or suzme (strained yogurt, see p.182)
- 3 garlic cloves, crushed
- 8 fresh mint sprigs, finely chopped
- 4 tablespoons olive oil

TO SERVE

- 16 baby gem lettuce leaves

Mix together the seven spices.

TO COOK THE BEEF

In a large, nonstick pan, heat the olive oil and sauté the onion for 2–3 minutes over medium heat. Add the ground beef and brown for 5 minutes. Sprinkle in the seven-spice mixture and cook for a further 8 minutes, stirring all the time. Next, add the zucchinis, cover the pan, and cook for a final 10 minutes. Season and stir in the fresh mint.

TO MAKE THE SAUCE

Simply combine all the ingredients in a bowl.

TO SERVE

Spoon the beef and zucchinis onto the individual lettuce leaves, and top with the garlic and yogurt sauce.

For 8 to share

Fig and Ricotta Tartlets
with Rose Petal Syrup

2/3 cup/150ml water

4 tablespoons superfine sugar

1 tablespoon dried rose petals

8 fresh ripe figs, quartered

zest of 1 orange

3½oz/100g shelled almonds

8 large sheets of filo pastry

4–6 tablespoons melted butter,
for brushing

9oz/250g ricotta, drained

TO SERVE

handful of fresh rose petals

Preheat the oven to 400°F (350°F fan)/200°C (180°C fan).

In a small pan, combine the water with the superfine sugar and dried rose petals, then gently bring to a boil. Reduce to a simmer and stir until the sugar has dissolved. Add the figs and orange zest and simmer for a further 5 minutes, until it turns to a thick syrup. Drain the fruit and reserve the syrup. Add the almonds to the fruit and allow to cool.

Lay a sheet of filo pastry on your work surface and brush all over with melted butter. Lay a second sheet on top, and again brush with butter. Repeat with 2 more sheets, then cut the 4 sheets into 8 equal squares. Repeat the process with the other 4 sheets of filo so that you have a total of 16 filo squares.

Spoon some ricotta onto each square and top with the fig and almond mixture. Make parcels out of the squares by lifting each corner of the pastry and pinching the edges. Leave a gap at the top.

Arrange the tartlets on a tray, brush with the remaining butter and bake in the oven for 12–15 minutes, until just golden. Remove and drizzle with the rose petal syrup. Scatter with some rose petals and serve.

Makes 16

Essential Accompaniments
& Spice Blends

Black Sesame Crisp Flatbread

½ tablespoon/5g fresh baker's
yeast, or 1 teaspoon/3g
active dry yeast

4–5 tablespoons warm water

5 tablespoons olive oil

1 cup/150g bread flour
flour, for dusting

3 tablespoons olive oil, extra
for brushing

1 tablespoon black sesame
seeds

TO SERVE

orange blossom honey

In a small bowl, stir the yeast into the warm water, then add the olive oil. Sift the flour into a separate bowl and pour in the yeasty water. Keep mixing until it turns to dough. Shape the dough into a ball and knead on a floured surface for 10 minutes, until it is nice and flexible. Shape into a ball and rest in a warm place in a covered bowl for 2 hours, until it has risen and doubled in size.

Preheat the oven to 425°F (400°F fan)/220°C (200°C fan).

Beat down the dough ball and knead again before splitting it into golf ball-sized pieces. With a rolling pin on a floured surface, roll each piece out until very thin. Brush with the extra olive oil, sprinkle with the sesame seeds, and arrange on a baking sheet. Bake in the oven for 20 minutes, until just golden (see picture, p.123). If you prefer, you can cook on a pizza stone.

Break into pieces and serve accompanied by the honey.

For 8 to share

Jerusalem Artichoke and Tahini Hummus

This hummus is made from Jerusalem artichokes instead of chickpeas, making the dish lighter.

1lb/450g Jerusalem artichokes, peeled and chopped

2 tablespoons tahini

2 garlic cloves, crushed

4 tablespoons lemon juice

3 teaspoons cumin seeds, toasted and ground

6 tablespoons olive oil

Place the Jerusalem artichokes in a pan and cover with cold water. Bring to a boil and cook on medium heat for 12–15 minutes, until soft. Drain and cool.

Purée the artichokes in a food processor. Add the tahini, garlic, lemon juice, and cumin. Switch your machine to pulse, then gradually drizzle in the oil and season.

For 8 to share

Eggplant and Tahini Dip

2 medium eggplants

2 garlic cloves, crushed

1 tablespoon olive oil

juice of ½ lemon

TO SERVE

1 tablespoon tahini

½ teaspoon sumac

½ red onion, finely chopped

Preheat the oven to 425°F (400°F fan)/220°C (200°C fan).

Place the whole eggplants on a baking tray and roast in the oven for 35–40 minutes, until cooked and soft, or chargrill on the stovetop (see method on p. 56). Once cool enough to handle, peel off the skin and blend in a food processor to a smooth purée. Add the garlic, olive oil, and lemon and blend again.

To serve, spoon into a bowl, drizzle with the tahini and sprinkle with the sumac and chopped onion.

For 8 to share

Baharat Nine Spice Blend

This is a wonderfully warming and aromatic blend of spices that can be added to soups, tomato sauces, lentils, and pilafs, and rubbed on fish, poultry, and meat. Mix it with a little olive oil and it can be used as a marinade too. It can also be combined with sumac, saffron, and turmeric. The proportions of the spices used in a baharat vary depending on whom you ask, but here's my special nine spice blend.

3 teaspoons mustard seeds

3 tablespoons coriander seeds

3 teaspoons fennel seeds

2 cinnamon sticks

3 teaspoons ground nutmeg

3 tablespoons cumin seeds

6 tablespoons dried thyme

6 tablespoons dried oregano

3 teaspoons black peppercorns

In a dry pan, toast the mustard, coriander, fennel, and cumin seeds, along with the cinnamon sticks, on high heat for 2–3 minutes then cool. Transfer to a bowl and add the rest of the ingredients. Using a mortar and pestle, crush to the consistency of coarse breadcrumbs. Mix well then store in a jar for up to 3 months.

Makes 30 tablespoons

Basic Skordalia

Skordalia is a Greek garlicky sauce or dip, usually made from either potatoes or bread.

2 slices of white bread, crusts removed

7oz/200g ground almonds

4 garlic cloves, crushed

¾ cup/200ml olive oil

juice of 1 lemon

Soak the bread in a bowl of water for 1 minute. Squeeze the bread dry and place in a food processor with the almonds and garlic. Process, drizzling in the olive oil, until you get a smooth and creamy consistency. Add the lemon juice and season to taste. If you prefer a thinner consistency, add about ¼–½ cup/50–100ml vegetable or meat stock.

Makes approx. 1¼ cups/300ml

Hummus

My hummus has always been deliciously light, silky, and creamy (a nod to modesty here), laboriously made with chickpeas that have had their skins removed. An extremely tiresome job, but I believed it to be the best and only way to do it. Muhanad Jazier, chef at the Sednaya in Syria, showed me how wrong I was. So get out the baking soda and a quantity of ice cubes, because you'll need them for this inspired method!

1lb/450g *dried chickpeas, soaked overnight*

¼ *tablespoon baking soda*

4–5 *ice cubes*

4 *tablespoons tahini*

2 *garlic cloves, crushed*

juice of 1 lemon

Drain the chickpeas and place them in a pan of fresh water. Add the baking soda and bring to a boil, then continue to simmer on low heat until the chickpeas are soft. You will need to skim the top of the water from time to time.

Drain the chickpeas and put a tablepoonful of them to one side. Blend the rest of the chickpeas in a food processor, dropping in the ice cubes one by one. This method produces a wonderfully smooth texture and turns the hummus almost white.

Transfer the blended chickpeas into a bowl, add the tahini (here I've used 4 tablespoons, but if you prefer a less nutty flavor, use less), garlic, and lemon juice, and season. Add a little more water if a thinner consistency is preferred.

Serve topped with the chickpeas put aside earlier.

For 10 to share

Pomegranate Molasses

This is a thick syrup made by boiling down pomegranate juice and sugar. It is sweet and sour at the same time. Delicious as a dressing, for marinating meat, or added to slow-cooked stews. Fairly readily available, but easy to make at home.

4 cups/1 liter pomegranate juice (from a carton)

½ cup/115g sugar

4 tablespoons lemon juice

In a large, uncovered saucepan, on medium heat, stir all the ingredients until the sugar has completely dissolved. Reduce the heat to a simmer and cook for roughly an hour, or until the juice has a syrupy consistency and has reduced to about a quarter. Pour into a jar, allow to cool, then store in the refrigerator for up to 4 weeks.

Makes 1 cup/250ml

Pesto

1 large bunch of fresh basil

2 garlic cloves

3½oz/100g pine nuts

7oz/200g Parmesan cheese, grated

scant ½ cup/100ml olive oil

Place the basil, garlic, pine nuts, and Parmesan in a food processor and season. Then, while blending, drizzle in the olive oil until you have a smooth paste.

Makes approx. 8 tablespoons

Tahini, Sumac, and Lemon Sauce

4 tablespoons tahini

grated zest and juice of a small lemon

1 garlic clove, crushed

½ tablespoon ground sumac

3 tablespoons olive oil

½ cup/120ml water

Place the tahini in a food processor, add the lemon zest and juice, along with the garlic and sumac. Process, adding the olive oil and water until you get a thin, cream-like consistency. Season to taste.

Makes 1 cup/250ml

Almond and Cumin Dukkah

Dukkah is an Egyptian spice and nut blend that has a fantastic crunchy texture.
Here I've mixed the dukkah with olive oil: a fantastic blend of flavors, perfect
in soups.

2oz/50g whole almonds, toasted	Place all the ingredients in a food processor and blend until well combined. I prefer a coarse consistency.
1 tablespoon coriander seeds, toasted	
½ tablespoon cumin seeds, toasted	
¼ tablespoon fennel seeds, toasted	
1 teaspoon black sesame seeds	

Makes 2oz/50g

Tahini and Cumin Dressing

3 tablespoons tahini	Blend together the tahini, lemon zest and juice, garlic, and cumin in a food processor. Slowly drizzle in the olive oil and water until you achieve a consistency like cream. Season to taste.
zest and juice of 1 small lemon	
1 garlic clove, crushed	
1 teaspoon cumin seeds, toasted and ground	
3 tablespoons olive oil	
scant ½ cup/100ml water	

Makes ¾ cup/200ml

Tahini Mayonnaise

3 egg yolks

²/₃ cup/150ml peanut oil

²/₃ cup/150ml olive oil

1 tablespoon tahini

juice of ½ lemon

Whisk the egg yolks in a bowl, then, still whisking, slowly drizzle in the peanut oil and olive oil until you have a thick mayonnaise consistency. Add the tahini and lemon, and season to taste.

Makes 1½ cups/350ml

Tomato and Sumac Dressing

Simple and quick, this will brighten any fresh green salad.

1 large ripe tomato, skinned and very finely chopped

2 tablespoons olive oil

1 shallot, grated

1 teaspoon runny honey

1 garlic clove, crushed

3 tablespoons white wine vinegar

½ tablespoon ground sumac

Combine all the ingredients in a bowl and season to taste.

For 8 to share

Yogurt, Mint, and Garlic Sauce

¾ cup/200ml yogurt

small bunch of fresh mint

1 garlic clove, crushed

2 tablespoons olive oil

handful of walnuts, finely chopped

Mix together the yogurt, mint, garlic, and olive oil. Transfer to a serving dish and sprinkle with the chopped walnuts.

For 8 to share

Za'atar at Quince

Both an herb in its own right and a blend of dried herbs. Za'atar, the herb has long green leaves and a thyme-like flavor. It is sometimes called wild thyme in English, and it grows along the slopes of the Syrian–Lebanese mountains. The za'atar referred to in this book, however, is the dried herb blend and I've included my signature recipe below. This is the main za'atar blend that I use at my restaurant, Quince.

4 teaspoons sesame seeds

4 tablespoons finely chopped fresh oregano

4 teaspoons dried marjoram

4 teaspoons ground sumac

1 teaspoon sea salt

4 teaspoons ground cumin

In a dry pan, lightly toast the sesame seeds on high heat for 1–2 minutes. Then place all the ingredients in a blender and process until finely mixed. Store in a jar in the fridge for up to a week.

Makes 6–8 tablespoons

Lemon Thyme Za'atar

8 fresh oregano sprigs, roughly torn, with flowers if possible

8 fresh lemon thyme sprigs, roughly torn

2 tablespoons sesame seeds

2 teaspoons ground sumac

½ teaspoon salt

2 teaspoons ground cumin

Simply combine all the ingredients. Store in a jar in the fridge for up to a week.

Makes 6–8 tablespoons

The Eastern Mediterranean Pantry

Aleppo chili pepper Mild, sweet, fruity, and slightly smoky. You might have to look around for it, but it is available in many Turkish and Middle Eastern food stores, in red and green variations, usually as dried flakes. You can substitute mild red chili flakes mixed with a bit of smoked paprika.

Almonds

Bulgur ground, cracked wheat grains

Cardamom Known as the "queen of the spices," cardamom is used in both savory and sweet cooking. You'll need both pods and ground.

Chickpeas Dried and canned.

Cinnamon (dried)

Coconut milk

Coconut (dried and shredded)

Coriander (ground and seeds)

Cumin (ground and seeds)

Extra virgin olive oil

Fennel (ground and seeds)

Ginger (dried)

Honey (runny)

Kadaifi This pastry is available in Middle Eastern and Turkish stores. It dries fast, so like filo pastry it must be kept under a damp cloth while you work with it.

Lavender (dried)

Marjoram (dried)

Mint (dried)

Mild chili pepper (flakes and powder)

Mustard (paste and seeds)

Nigella seeds These come from a flower that is a member of the buttercup family. They have a sharp, nutty, slightly peppery flavor. Make sure you toast them beforehand to release their flavors.

Nutmeg (ground)

Orange blossom water Also known as orange flower water. Orange flowers have a citrusy, bittersweet flavor and at the same time, warm caramel notes. As well as pastries and sweet dishes, it is also used with chicken, pumpkin, and in pilafs.

The secret is to use very little—too much and you will end up with a heavily perfumed dish.

Oregano (dried)

Orzo

Panko breadcrumbs These are readily available in most Asian food stores, but if you can't get hold of them, toast ordinary breadcrumbs so they have a crunch to them.

Paprika The true aristocrat of spices, from the noble sweet varieties to the fiercely hot. It is hardly surprising, seeing that they use so much of it, that many people give the Hungarians the credit for introducing paprika to European cuisine, but it was in fact the Turks, via their trade routes, and from there to Hungary by way of the Balkans, who introduced the pepper to the Hungarians in the middle of the sixteenth century.

Parsley (dried)

Peppercorns (black and green)

Pine nuts

Pistachios Buy them whole, shelled, and unsalted.

Ras-el-hanout A Moroccan spice blend usually made up of black pepper, coriander, ginger, paprika, allspice, cardamom, mace, nutmeg, turmeric, cayenne, cloves and rose petals. Available to buy in supermarkets and Middle Eastern stores, or make your own.

Rose water

Saffron Can be bought in the form of threads, powder, and liquid. Threads are the most expensive; a pinch of saffron is roughly 12 threads.

Sea salt

Sesame seeds Very high in oil content, with a nutty aroma. They're used to make za'atar, tahini, and helva. You'll also need black sesame seeds for some of the recipes.

Sumac You'll see that this is a key ingredient for many of my recipes and fortunately it's more widely available now. Any good Middle Eastern food store will sell it crushed or ground, and some supermarkets stock it now. Sumac is the edible berry of a tree related to the mango. Sumac berries turn from dark pink to purple as they ripen, and as they dry and harden, they become the size of peppercorns. Sumac has a fruity aroma and citrusy flavor. Great with fish, salads, and in pilafs.

Suzme (labne) Suzme is strained yogurt, known in the Middle East as labne. When yogurt is strained and the mixture drains away, it becomes very thick. Left for twenty-four to forty-eight hours, it takes on the texture of cream cheese, thereby allowing it to be rolled in a variety of coatings, such as herbs, nuts, and seeds. You should use a good-quality, full-fat plain yogurt without additives. Prepare the suzme 1 or 2 days in advance of cooking with it. Place the yogurt in the center of some double-layered muslin or cheesecloth (approximately 12 × 12in/ 30 × 30cm in size). Standing at a sink, twist the muslin around the yogurt until you have a tight ball. Tie the top with some string and suspend the ball (I tie it to the faucet) for a day or so. You will end up with yogurt of a very thick consistency. It will be roughly half the weight you started with.

Tahini Sesame paste, used widely in eastern Mediterranean and Middle Eastern cuisines.

Walnuts

Yufka Thin sheets of pre-cooked pastry, not dissimilar to filo, used in the cuisines of Turkey, Syria, and Greece. Available in Middle Eastern or Polish stores, or online.

Index

Acknowledgements

What can I say about Jonathan Lovekin: a fantastic photographer and great friend, an integral part of making my cookbooks what they are.

It is one thing having a great idea, and quite another to put it into action: Caroline Gascoigne was the woman for the job. Thank you for your belief and attention to detail, without which this book would not have been as beautiful as it is.

I had always wanted to work with Susie Theodorou, one of the best stylists in the business, and I wasn't disappointed: great job.

Richard Marston I thank too: the design of *Orient Express* is pure class and elegance!

Natali of James Knight fishmongers: delicious fish and seafood, and she has always been there for me!

Last, but not least, thanks to Emma Rose, for coming back to help with the editing of this book. You know my work so well now!

First American edition published 2013 by

INTERLINK BOOKS
An imprint of Interlink Publishing Group, Inc.
46 Crosby Street, Northampton, MA 01060
www.interlinkbooks.com

Library of Congress Cataloging-in-Publication Data

Rowe, Silvena.
Orient express : fast food from the Eastern Mediterranean / by Silvena Rowe ;
photography by Jonathan Lovekin. -- First American edition.
pages cm
Includes index.
ISBN 978-1-56656-918-7
1. Cooking, Middle Eastern. 2. Cooking, Mediterranean. I. Title.
TX725.M628R688 2012
641.591822--dc23
2012032361

Commissioning Editor: Emma Rose
Designer: Richard Marston
Cover designer: Emma Grey
Production: Phil Brown
Stylist: Susie Theodorou
Copyeditor: Annie Lee
American edition editor: Leyla Moushabeck

Printed and bound in China